THE BOOK OF
POISONOUS
QUOTES

Compiled by Colin M. Jarman

CB
CONTEMPORARY BOOKS

Library of Congress Cataloging-in-Publication Data

The book of poisonous quotes / compiled by Colin M. Jarman.
    p.   cm.
Includes index.
ISBN 0-8092-3681-8
    1. Quotations, English.   I.   Jarman, Colin M., 1958–
PN6081.G83   1993
082—dc20   93-34513
                                                                        CIP

Cover illustration by Mark Anderson

Published by Contemporary Books
A division of NTC/Contemporary Publishing Group, Inc.
4255 West Touhy Avenue
Lincolnwood (Chicago), Illinois 60712-1975 U.S.A.
Printed in the United States of America
International Standard Book Number: 0-8092-3681-8

00 01 02 03 04 05 LB 22 21 20 19 18 17 16 15 14 13 12 11 10

CONTENTS

INTRODUCTION

Beauty is only skin deep.
But ugly goes clear to the bone.

A. B. Evans

And so it is with poisonous quotes—a little bit of praise may go a long way, but insults go on forever.

This *Book of Poisonous Quotes* has thousands of choice cutting criticisms and willfully wicked witticisms to choose from. Nobody is safe from these stinging salvos—pillars of society are pilloried, authors written off, sports stars run down, celebrities defamed, financiers discredited, and actors hamstrung.

My propensity for things poisonous started back in 1987, when I was told by a sports editor that I could not call the (yet-to-be-disgraced) Canadian athlete Ben Johnson a "human cheetah." Ever since that letdown over a put-down I have been in search of my personal Holy Grail—the perfect (or perfectly acceptable) insult. Six years of research have led me to believe that the perfect put-down has not yet been uttered—but there has never been a shortage of people who have tried to discover the aqua regia of acrimony. A year's

1

research in the United States left me with the impression that the American Uncivil War was still being fought—between commentator and politician, critic and artist, reviewer and author.

In their traditional evening-wear battle dress and fueled by a proud motto ("The pen is mightier than the sword"), the critical snide snipers have always had their sights firmly set on their favorite targets—be it a Nixon, a Streisand, or a Whitman.

This war of the words is not a one-sided combat zone. Critics with bitchy trigger fingers may draw first blood, but they are not sheltered from hostile fire being returned. Reviewers may go over the top from the comfort of their own writing desks, but the likes (or dislikes) of Rich, Simon, Mencken, and Woollcott are constantly shelled with the repercussions of their own critical fallout.

> You can't say civilization don't advance—for every war they kill you a new way.
>
> *Will Rogers*

And so it is with poisonous quotes—civilization advances with a new crossbreed of critic, a new strain of reviewer, and a new generation of Grouchos—after all,

> The tongue is the only instrument that gets sharper with use.
> *Washington Irving*

—Colin Jarman

HOW TO USE
THIS BOOK

The Book of Poisonous Quotes has been compiled to be used as either reading or reference material.

The table of contents lists the subsections within the major categories.

Within the sections, the quotations are listed alphabetically by individual subject or, if there is no individual subject, by source. Within each subsection, the quotations are listed alphabetically by source.

The index contains the names of the subjects of the quotations as well as the names of the people quoted.

Biographical details include birth and death dates, if known. This information is given to place the quotes in a time context rather than in the interests of providing a definitive biographical reference.

Sections containing reviews are alphabetically listed in two fashions—either by reviewer or by subject as indicated in the table of contents.

1
CRITICS AND CRITICISM

GENERAL

A critic is a man who writes about things he doesn't like.

Anonymous

The most important critic is Time.

Anonymous

Critics are the stupid who discuss the wise.

Anonymous

Criticism is the disapproval of people, not for having faults but for having faults different from ours.

Anonymous

American critics are like American universities. They both have dull and half-dead faculties.

Edward Albee (1969)

Critics are like eunuchs in a harem. They're there every night, they see it done every night, they see how it should be done every night, but they can't do it themselves.

Brendan Behan

Critics are eunuchs at a gang-bang.

George Burns

To an anonymous critic—Thou eunuch of language; thou pimp of gender, murderous accoucheur of infant learning, thou pickle-herring in the puppet show nonsense.

Robert Burns

In judging others, folks will work overtime for no pay.

Charles Carruthers

I do not resent criticism, even when, for the sake of emphasis, it parts for the time with reality.

Winston Churchill (1941)

I love criticism just so long as it's unqualified praise.

Noël Coward

It would be nice if sometimes the kind of things I say were considered worthy of quotation. It isn't difficult, you know, to be witty or amusing when one has something to say that is destructive, but damned hard to be clever and quotable when you are singing someone's praises.

Noël Coward

Taking to pieces is the trade of those who cannot construct.

Ralph Waldo Emerson

Any fool can criticize, and many of them do.

C. Garbett

A critic is a man created to praise greater men than himself, but he is never able to find them.

Richard Le Gallienne

Critics are probably more prone to clichés than fiction writers who pluck things out of the air.

Penelope Gilliatt

Don't pay any attention to the critics—don't even ignore them.

Samuel Goldwyn

A good review from the critics is just another stay of execution.

Dustin Hoffman

To escape criticism—do nothing, say nothing, be nothing.

Elbert Hubbard

One gets tired of the role critics are supposed to have in this culture: It's like being the piano player in a whorehouse; you don't have any control over the action going on upstairs.

Robert Hughes,
'Publishers Weekly' (1986)

Mediocrity is more dangerous in a critic than in a writer.

Eugene Ionesco (1966)

I find the pain of a little censure, even when it is unfounded, is more acute than the pleasure of much praise.

Thomas Jefferson

Honest criticism is hard to take, particularly from a relative, a friend, an acquaintance, or a stranger.

Franklin P. Jones

In the arts, the critic is the only independent source of information. The rest is advertising.

Pauline Kael,
'Newsweek' (1973)

For critics, I care the five-hundred-thousandth part of the tithe of a half-farthing.

Charles Lamb (1830)

I won't quit [acting] until I get run over by a truck, a producer, or a critic.

Jack Lemmon (1986)

I never read bad reviews about myself because my best friends invariably tell me about them.

Oscar Levant

A critic is one who goes along for deride.

L. L. Levinson

He has a right to criticize, who has a heart to help.

Abraham Lincoln

Freedom to criticize is held to compensate for the freedom to err—this is the American system.

Mary McCarthy

Criticism is prejudice made plausible.

H. L. Mencken

I've always felt those articles somehow reveal more about the writers than they do about me.

Marilyn Monroe

A bad review is even less important than whether it is raining in Patagonia.

Iris Murdoch

The better and more honest a critic you are, the fewer friends will eventually send flowers to the funeral parlor.

George Jean Nathan

Insects sting, not from malice but because they want to live. It is the same with critics—they desire our blood, not pain.

*Friedrich Nietzsche,
'Miscellaneous Maxims
and Opinions' (1879)*

Critics?—I love every bone in their heads.

Eugene O'Neill

Critics are a dissembling, dishonest, contemptible race of men. Asking a working writer what he feels about critics is like asking a lamppost what he feels about dogs.

John Osborne

The trouble with most of us is that we would rather be ruined by praise than saved by criticism.

Norman Vincent Peale

A critic is someone who's at his best when you're at your worst.

Tony Pettito

As for you, little envious Prigs, snarling, bastard, puny Criticks, you'll soon have railed your last: Go hang yourself.

François Rabelais

Can't a critic give his opinion of an omelette without being asked to lay an egg?

Clayton Rawson

All critics should be assassinated.

>   *Man Ray*

A critic is a man whose watch is five minutes ahead of other people's watches.

>   *Charles Sainte-Beuve*

Critics are like mayors of New York; nobody really wants to like them.

>   *Dore Schary*

Critics, like other people, see what they look for, not what is actually before them.

>   *George Bernard Shaw*

Contemporary criticism only represents the amount of ignorance genius has to contend with.

>   *Percy Bysshe Shelley*

Time is the only critic without ambition.

>   *John Steinbeck*

A bad review is like baking a cake with all the best ingredients and having someone sit on it.

>   *Danielle Steel*

A critic is a man who knows the way but can't drive the car.

Kenneth Tynan

They search for ages for the wrong word, which, to give them credit, they eventually find.

Peter Ustinov (1952)

Really to stop criticism they say one must die.

Voltaire, 'Les Trois Empereurs en Sorbonne'

Don't pay attention to bad reviews. Today's newspaper is tomorrow's toilet paper.

Jack Warner

CRITICS AT LARGE

Joseph Addison *(1672-1719)*
Damn with faint praise, assent with civil leer,
And without sneering teach the rest to sneer;
Willing to wound, and yet afraid to strike,
Just a hint a fault, and hesitate dislike;
Alike reserv'd to blame or to commend,
A tim'rous foe, and a suspicious friend.

Alexander Pope

Max Beerbohm   *(1872–1956)*
The gods have bestowed on Max the gift of perpetual old age.

> *Oscar Wilde*

Robert Benchley   *(1889–1945)*
Robert Benchley has a style that is weak and lies down frequently to rest.

> *Max Eastman,*
> *'Enjoyment of Laughter'*

An enchanting toad of a man.

> *Helen Hayes*

J. Churton Collins   *(1848–1908)*
A louse in the locks of literature.

> *Alfred, Lord Tennyson*

Clive James   *(b 1939)*
Not satire, but name-dropping. He writes like a man who wishes he was invited to more parties.

> *Paul Theroux, 'The Sunday*
> *(London) Times' (1981)*

Randall Jarrell   *(1914–65)*
If God were a writer and wrote a book that Randall did not think was good, Randall would not have hesitated

to give it a bad review. And if God complained, Randall would then set about showing God what was wrong with his sentences.

Robert Watson

Samuel Johnson   *(1709-84)*
The pompous preacher of melancholy moralities.

Jeremy Bentham

The Caliban of literature.

Gilbert Cowper

A dangerous person to disagree with.

T. S. Eliot

There is no arguing with Johnson; for when his pistol misses fire, he knocks you down with the butt end of it.

Oliver Goldsmith

Pauline Kael   *(b 1919)*
Oh, f*** Pauline Kael, f*** her! And I don't use that language all the time. I don't care what she has to say. She's a bitch. She's spiteful, and she's wrong. Let's not talk about Pauline Kael.

George Cukor

Pauline Kael is the Rambo of film critics . . . a demented bag lady.

Alan Parker (1990)

H. L. Mencken   *(1880–1956)*
He edited a magazine called *The Smart Set*, which is like calling Cape Kennedy "Lover's Lane."

Ben Hecht,
'Letter from Bohemia'

What he believed in and what his readers wanted to be told were soon indistinguishable; his work became a series of circus tricks, a perpetual search for some new object of middle-class culture to belabor and some new habit or caprice of *Homus Americanus* to ridicule.

Alfred Kazin,
'On Native Grounds'

George Jean Nathan   *(1882–1958)*
'Art of the Night' is the most valuable of his works on the theater . . . He can, in short, write. And so he makes almost all of the other dramatic commentators (I can think, in fact, of but three exceptions, and I'm not sure of two of those) look as if they spelled out their reviews with alphabet blocks.

Dorothy Parker,
'The New Yorker' (1928)

Dorothy Parker *(1893-1967)*
The belle dame sans merci has the ruthlessness of the
great tragic lyricists whose work was allegorized in the
fable of the nightingale singing with her breast against
a thorn. It is disillusion recollected in tranquillity
where the imagination has at last controlled the emo-
tions. It comes out clear, and with the authentic sparkle
of a great vintage.

Henry Seidel Canby

(This is popularly misquoted as a direct reference to Parker—
A nightingale singing with her breast against a thorn.*)*

(Also note lines of a Dorothy Parker poem:
His little trills and chirpings were his best,
No music like the nightingale's was born
Within his throat; but he, too, laid his breast
Upon a thorn.

Minor Poet)

Petite, pretty, and deadly as an asp.

Howard Teichmann

Her acidic bon mots were the olives of the martini age.

'Vanity Fair' (1986)

She has put into what she has written a voice, a state of
mind, an era, a few moments of human experience that
nobody else has conveyed.

Edmund Wilson

A combination of Little Nell and Lady Macbeth.

> *Alexander Woollcott,*
> *'While Rome Burns'*

Rex Reed   *(b 1939)*
Rex Reed is either at your feet or at your throat.

> *Ava Gardner*

All that bullshit with the New York critics is just cock-tail-party talk. I've become a multimillionaire with things that Rex Reed hated.

> *Jerry Weintraub (1975)*

Frank Rich   *(b 1949)*
Some days I want to kill Frank Rich. He represents this Great Deaf Ear I must somehow get through to in order to reach a theater-going public . . . the years have gone on and he's gotten harder and harder and harder.

> *Christopher Durang*

Frank Rich is a terrible critic. He's an unfortunate blot on the American theater . . . He's a boy, he's an untutored boy, who doesn't realize there's anything higher than his own perceptions. As Tolstoy said, "Mediocre men must of necessity have a mediocre idea of what constitutes greatness" and he was speaking of Mr. Rich when he wrote it.

David Mamet (1988)

Frank Rich and John Simon are the syphilis and gonorrhea of the theater.

David Mamet

George Bernard Shaw *(1856–1950)*
A freakish homunculus germinated outside lawful procreation.

Henry Arthur Jones

It is his life work to announce the obvious in terms of the scandalous.

H. L. Mencken

Intellectually he is beneath contempt. Artistically he appeals only to pseudophilosophers. Are we not all a little tired of this blatant self-puffery?

Alfred Noyes

A desiccated bourgeois, a fossilized chauvinist.

'Pravda'

As yet, Bernard Shaw hasn't become prominent enough to have any enemies; but none of his friends like him.

Oscar Wilde

John Simon   *(b 1925)*
You have to make important differences between critics and assassins. There are important differences between John Simon and Sirhan Sirhan. Sirhan Sirhan is in jail.

Rocco Landesman (1990)

Walter Winchell   *(1897-1972)*
I don't see why Walter Winchell is allowed to live.

Ethel Barrymore

He is more like some freak of climate—a tornado, say, or an electric storm that is heard whistling and roaring far away, against which everybody braces himself; and then it strikes and does its whirling damage.

Alistair Cooke,
'Listener' (1947)

Alexander Woollcott   *(1887-1943)*
Mr. W. was an emotionalist who rarely succumbed to the chill demands of logic. Woollcott was less a critic than an amusing hysteric.

Tallulah Bankhead

The smartest of Alecs.

Heywood Broun

Listening to Mr. Woollcott on the radio is like being hit with a cream puff; you are uninjured but rather sickened.

Robert Forsythe

He looked like something that had gotten loose from Macy's Thanksgiving Day Parade.

Harpo Marx

Old Vitriol and Violets.

James Thurber

He always praises the first production of each season, being reluctant to stone the first cast.

Walter Winchell

2
THE CREATIVE ARTS

ARCHITECTS AND ARCHITECTURE

An architect is two percent gentleman and ninety-eight percent renegade car salesman.

Anonymous

In my experience, if you have to keep the lavatory door shut by extending your left leg, it's modern architecture.

Nancy Banks-Smith,
'The Guardian' (1969)

Any work of architecture that does not express serenity is a mistake.

Luis Barragan,
'Time' (1980)

Modern architecture is a flop. There is no question that our cities are uglier today than they were fifty years ago.

Philip Johnson (1968)

Architects are pretty much high-class whores. We can turn down projects the way they turn down clients, but we've both got to say yes to someone if we want to stay in business.

Philip Johnson,
'Esquire' (1980)

Architecture is the art of how to waste space.

Philip Johnson

Architecture is too important to be left to architects alone. Like crime, it is a problem for society as a whole.

Berthold Lubetkin (1985)

Perhaps the blank faceless abstract quality of our modern architecture is a reflection of the anxiety we feel before the void, a kind of visual static which emanates from the psyche of us all, as if we do not know which way to go.

Norman Mailer,
'Cannibals and Christians'

On Le Corbusier's style—If I were building a house tomorrow, it would certainly not follow the lines of a dynamo or a steam shovel.

H. L. Mencken

The fundamental failure of modern architecture was that in the shift from an agrarian society to an industrialized society, from handicrafts to the machine, from single production to mass production, in trying to produce in abundance for all the people, the people themselves got left out.

John Portman (1984)

No architecture can be truly noble which is not imperfect.

John Ruskin

Suburbia is where the developer bulldozes out the trees, then names the streets after them.

Bill Vaughan

A doctor can bury his mistakes, but an architect can only advise his client to plant vines.

Frank Lloyd Wright

BUILDINGS AND MONUMENTS

Biltmore Hotel, Los Angeles
Patterned after an Italian Renaissance palace, it is eighty-eight times as large and one millionth as valuable to the continuation of man—the Pentagon of traveling salesmen.

Norman Mailer,
'Esquire' (1960)

Eiffel Tower, Paris
The Empire State Building after taxes.

Anonymous

A gigantic carrot that goes by the name of the Eiffel Tower.

Elena Blavatsky

Guggenheim Museum, New York
A war between architecture and painting in which both come out badly maimed.

John Canady,
'New York Times' (1959)

Heathrow Airport, London
I did not fully understand the dread term "terminal illness" until I saw Heathrow Airport for myself.

Dennis Potter

Hubert H. Humphrey Metrodome, Minneapolis

I don't like that Hubert H. Humphrey Metrodome. It's a shame a great guy like Humphrey had to be named after it.

Billy Martin

John F. Kennedy Center for the Performing Arts, Washington, D.C.

The building is a national tragedy—a cross between a concrete candy box and a marble sarcophagus in which the art of the architecture lies buried.

Ada Louise Huxtable
(1971)

National Theatre, London

The best view of London is from the National Theatre, because from there you can't see the National Theatre.

Anonymous

The Pyramids

As for the pyramids, there is nothing to wonder at in them so much as the fact that so many men could be found degraded enough to spend their lives constructing a tomb for some ambitious booby, whom it would have been wiser and manlier to have drowned in the Nile, and then given his body to the dogs.

Henry David Thoreau
(1854)

St. Peter's Basilica, Rome

As a whole St. Peter's is fit for nothing but a ballroom, and it is a little too gaudy even for that.

John Ruskin (1840)

Statue of Liberty, New York

You have set up in New York Harbor a monstrous idol which you call Liberty. The only thing that remains to complete the monument is to put on its pedestal the inscription written by Dante on the gate of Hell: "All hope abandon, ye who enter here."

George Bernard Shaw (1933)

Sydney Opera House

It looks like a typewriter full of oyster shells; like a broken Pyrex casserole dish in a brown cardboard box.

Clive James, 'The Observer' (1983)

The greatest public relations building since the pyramids.

Billy Wentworth

Vancouver City Hall

I declare this thing open, whatever it is.

Prince Philip

The Vatican
One of the best warehouses I ever saw.

> *Arnold Wesker, 'Chips with*
> *Everything' (1962)*

Washington Monument
Saw Washington Monument. Phallic. Appalling. A national catastrophe.

> *Arnold Bennett,*
> *'Journal' (1911)*

Windsor Castle
A stately pile from the outside, but in the interior one sees that the state apartments are decidedly shabby, like a second-class boardinghouse.

> *Lilian Leland,*
> *'Traveling Alone' (1890)*

FASHION

Her hat is a creation that will never go out of style. It will look ridiculous year after year.

> *Fred Allen*

If you read the papers, you will notice that no girl with short hair has made an advantageous marriage lately. So what's the sense of looking like a shaved bulldog?

Elizabeth Arden

On miniskirts—Never in the history of fashion has so little material been raised so high to reveal so much that needs to be covered so badly.

Sir Cecil Beaton (1969)

She was what we used to call a suicide blonde—dyed by her own hand.

Saul Bellow

The jean! The jean is the destructor! It is a dictator! It is destroying creativity. The jean must be stopped.

Pierre Cardin,
'People' (1976)

Saint-Laurent has excellent taste. The more he copies me, the better taste he displays.

Coco Chanel (1971)

Art produces ugly things which frequently become beautiful with time. Fashion, on the other hand, produces beautiful things which always become ugly with time.

Jean Cocteau

Fashionability is a kind of vulgarity.

George Darley

Fashion exists for women with no taste, etiquette for people with no breeding.

Queen Marie of Romania (1938)

If women dressed for men, the stores wouldn't sell much—just an occasional sun visor!

Groucho Marx

A kilt is an unrivaled garment for fornication and diarrhea.

John Masters

Fashion is an imposition, a rein on freedom.

Golda Meir

Princess Di wears more clothes in one day than Gandhi wore in his whole life.

Joan Rivers

A dress has no purpose unless it makes a man want to take it off.

Françoise Sagan

Why not be oneself? That is the whole secret of successful appearance. If one is a greyhound, why try to look like a Pekinese?

Dame Edith Sitwell

Conformism is so hot on the heels of the mass-produced avant-garde that the "ins" and "outs" change places with the speed of mach 3.

Igor Stravinsky

Distrust any enterprise that requires new clothes.

Henry David Thoreau

Every generation laughs at the old fashions but follows religiously the new.

Henry David Thoreau

If you have to talk about fashion, then you are not in it.

Michaele Vollbracht

There will be little change in men's pockets this year.

'Wall Street Journal' (1948)

Fashion is the method by which the fantastic becomes for a moment universal.

Oscar Wilde

PAINTING

Modern art is like trying to follow the plot in alphabet soup.

Anonymous

Modern art is when you buy a picture to cover a hole in the wall and then decide the hole looks much better.

Anonymous

A modern artist is one who throws paint on a canvas, wipes it off with a cloth, and sells the cloth.

Anonymous

One reassuring thing about modern art is that things can't possibly be as bad as they are painted.

Anonymous

Pop art is the indelible raised to the unspeakable.

Leonard Baskin

What is art? Prostitution.

Charles Baudelaire

Most of those who call themselves artists are in reality picture dealers, only they make the pictures themselves.

Samuel Butler

Abstract art is a product of the untalented, sold by the unprincipled to the utterly bewildered.

Al Capp,
'National Observer' (1963)

An artist cannot speak about his art any more than a plant can discuss horticulture.

John Cocteau (1955)

One sees a square lady with three breasts and a guitar up her crotch.

Noël Coward

The real meaning of this Cubist movement is nothing else than the total destruction of the art of painting.

Kenyon Cox,
'Harper's Weekly' (1913)

I can't tell what those new painters are saying,
Although to some they're the new sensation,
As on canvas they keep throwing or spraying
The pigment of their imagination.

Leonard Dittell

Art is a jealous mistress.

Ralph Waldo Emerson,
'Conduct of Life'

Art is either plagiarism or revolution.

Paul Gauguin

A work of art is an exaggeration.

André Gide

All profoundly original art looks ugly at first.

Clement Greenberg

I have generally found that persons who had studied painting least were the best judges of it.

William Hogarth (1761)

If you could say it in words there would be no reason to paint.

Edward Hopper

If debased art is kitsch, perhaps kitsch redeemed by honest vulgarity may become art.

Pauline Kael

The more minimal the art the more maximum the explanation.

Hilton Kramer

I can truthfully say that the painter has observed the Ten Commandments. Because he hath not made to himself the likeness of anything in heaven above, or that which is on earth beneath, or that which is in the water under the earth.

Abraham Lincoln

Art for art's sake makes no more sense then gin for gin's sake.

W. Somerset Maugham

Finding a businessman interested in the arts is like finding chicken shit in the chicken salad.

Alice Neel

How vain painting is—we admire the realistic depiction of objects which in their original state we don't admire at all.

Blaise Pascal,
'Pensées' (1670)

Everyone wants to understand painting. Why don't they try to understand the singing of the birds? People love the night, a flower, everything which surrounds them without trying to understand them. But painting—that they *must* understand.

Pablo Picasso

An artist should be fit for the best society and keep out of it.

John Ruskin

A portrait is a painting with something wrong with the mouth.

John Singer Sargent

If more than ten percent of the population likes a painting it should be burned, for it must be bad.

George Bernard Shaw

The true artist will let his wife starve, his children go barefoot, his mother drudge for his living at seventy, sooner than work at anything but his art.

George Bernard Shaw

An artist has been defined as a neurotic who continually cures himself with his art.

Lee Simonson

This is either a forgery or a damn clever original.

Frank Sullivan

The immature artist imitates. Mature artists steal.

Lionel Trilling

If that's art, I'm a Hottentot!

Harry S. Truman

I'm glad the old masters are all dead, and I only wish they had died sooner.

Mark Twain

Visiting museums bastardizes the personality, just as hobnobbing with the priests makes you lose your faith.

Maurice Vlaminck

An artist is someone who produces things that people don't need to have but that he—for some good reason—thinks it would be a good idea to give them.

Andy Warhol

Two and two continue to make four, in spite of the whine of the amateur for three, or the cry of the art critic for five.

James McNeill Whistler

There are three kinds of people in the world: those who can't stand Picasso, those who can't stand Raphael, and those who've never heard of either of them.

John White

A work of art is useless. So is a flower.

Oscar Wilde

Bad artists always admire each other's work.

Oscar Wilde

There are moments when art attains almost the dignity of manual labor.

Oscar Wilde

PAINTERS

Anonymous
They couldn't find the artist, so they hung the picture.

Anonymous

Aubrey Beardsley   *(1872-98)*
His was a passing fad, a little sign of decadence and nothing more.

'New York Times' (1898)

Duabaway Weirdsley.

'Punch' (1895)

A face like a silver hatchet, with grass green hair.

Oscar Wilde

Georges Braque   *(1882-1963)*
He constructs deformed metallic men of a terrible simplification. He is contemptuous of form, reduces everything, sites and figures and house, to schemes, to cubes.

Louis Vauxcelles,
'Gil Blas' (1908)

(This quote is attributed as the first reference to Cubism.)

Paul Cézanne   *(1839-1906)*

I began a happening in New York by announcing in front of three thousand spectators that Cézanne was a catastrophe of awkwardness—a painter of decrepit structures of the past. I was applauded, principally because nobody knew who Cézanne was.

Salvador Dali

To me, apples are fruit—to Cézanne they were mountains!

David Smith

Salvador Dali   *(1904-89)*

Faced with a virtual complete record of the old phony's unswerving bathos, it was impossible not to burst out yawning . . . the uproar of banality numbed the mind.

Clive James,
'Flying Visits' (1984)

Señor Dali, born delirious,
Considers it folly to be serious.

Phyllis McGinley (1960)

The naked truth about me is to the naked truth about Salvador Dali as an old ukelele in the attic is to a piano in a tree, and I mean a piano with breasts.

> *James Thurber,*
> *'Merry-Go-Round' (1945)*

Edgar Degas   *(1834–1917)*
He is nothing but a peeping Tom, behind the coulisses, and among the dressing rooms of ballet dancers, noting only travesties of fallen womanhood, most disgusting and offensive.

> *'The Churchman' (1886)*

Paul Gauguin   *(1848–1903)*
Don't talk to me of Gauguin. I'd like to wring the fellow's neck.

> *Paul Cézanne*

A decorator tainted with insanity.

> *Kenyon Cox, 'Harper's*
> *Weekly' (1913)*

Vincent van Gogh   *(1853–90)*
Vincent van Gogh's mother painted all of his best things. The famous mailed decapitated ear was a figment of the public relations firm engaged by van Gogh's dealer.

> *Roy Blount, Jr.*

Peter Hurd *(b 1904)*
On his portrait—The ugliest thing I ever saw.

Lyndon B. Johnson

Paul Klee *(1879-1940)*
His pictures seem to resemble not pictures but a sample book of patterns of linoleum.

Cyril Asquith

Roy Lichtenstein *(b 1923)*
The worst artist in the U.S. *'Life'*

Edouard Manet *(1832-83)*
You are the first in the decadence of your art.

Charles Baudelaire

'Déjeuner sur l'Herbe'—Is this drawing? Is this painting? I see garments without feeling the anatomical structure that supports them and explains their movements. I see boneless fingers and heads without skulls. I see side-whiskers made of two strips of black cloth that could have been glued to the cheeks. What else do I see? The artist's lack of conviction and sincerity.

Jules Castaganry, 'Salons'

'The Absinthe Drinker'—There is only one absinthe drinker, and that's the man who painted this idiotic picture.

Thomas Couture (1860)

Henri Matisse *(1869–1954)*
Matisse is an unmitigated bore. Surely the vogue of those twisted and contorted human figures must be as short as it is artificial.

Harriet Monroe,
'Chicago Tribune' (1913)

Before buying 'Woman with Hat'—It was a tremendous effort on his part, a thing brilliant and powerful, but the nastiest smear of paint I had ever seen.

Leo Stein (1947)

Michelangelo *(1475–1564)*
If Michelangelo had been a heterosexual, the Sistine Chapel would have been painted basic white and with a roller.

Rita Mae Brown (1988)

He was a good man but he did not know how to paint.

El Greco

Claude Monet   *(1840–1926)*
It is only too easy to catch people's attention by doing something worse than anyone else has dared to do it before.

Charivari

A skillful but short-lived decorator.

Edgar Degas (1888)

Edvard Munch   *(1863–1944)*
He might perhaps as well have been a criminal as an artist, and the hand which applied colors to the canvas in this way might have been equally capable of wielding a knife or throwing a bomb.

F. X. Salda

Pablo Picasso   *(1881–1973)*
A Catalan wizard who fools with shapes.

Bernard Berenson

Picasso kept finding new ways of avoiding maturity.

Clive James, 'Flying Visits' (1984)

If I met Picasso in the street I would kick him in the pants.

> *Sir Alfred Munnings,*
> *speech at the Royal*
> *Academy (1949)*

'*Still Life with a Bull's Head*'—My little granddaughter of six could do as well.

> *Norman Rockwell*

Jackson Pollock   *(1912–56)*

Pollock does not seem to be especially talented, there being too much of an air of baked macaroni about some of his patterns, as though they were scrambled baroque designs.

> *Parker Tyler, 'View' (1945)*

Auguste Renoir   *(1841–1919)*

On the work of M. Auguste Renoir it is hard to speak with gravity. A glance at some of the canvases which bear his name will explain more fully than any words of mine the difficulty one might experience in taking such work seriously.

> *Philip Burne-Jones (1905)*

Dante Gabriel Rossetti   *(1828–82)*

The Rossetti Exhibition—I have been to it and am pleased to find it more odious than I even dared to hope.

> *Samuel Butler*

I should say that Rossetti was a man without any principles at all, who earnestly desired to find some means of salvation along the lines of least resistance.

Ford Madox Ford,
'Ancient Lights'

Henri Rousseau   *(1844-1910)*
He had enthusiasm, faith in his art of painting, and also the instinctive qualities that are lacking in so many conquering heroes of the Salon. Unfortunately, taste, measure, everything that constitutes talent are missing.

'Le Mercure de France'
(1910)

Peter Paul Rubens   *(1577-1640)*
To my eye Rubens's coloring is most contemptible. His shadows are of a filthy brown somewhat the color of excrement.

William Blake (1808)

John Singer Sargent   *(1856-1925)*
It is positively dangerous to sit next to Sargent. It is taking your face in your hands.

Anonymous

Graham Sutherland *(1903-80)*
Portrait of Sir Winston Churchill—It makes me look
as if I was straining a stool.

Winston Churchill

Tintoretto *(1518-94)*
He will never be anything but a dauber.

Titian

Titian *(1477-1576)*
If I hear the name Titian, I have to lie down.

Helen Bell

Henri de Toulouse-Lautrec *(1864-1901)*
A tiny blacksmith with little eye-glasses.

Jules Renard

A baron who has taken root in a brothel.

André Suare

Leonardo da Vinci *(1452-1519)*
Leonardo da Vinci did everything and did nothing very
well.

Marie Bashkirtseef,
'Journal' (1883)

He bores me. He ought to have stuck to his flying machines.

Auguste Renoir

Andy Warhol *(1930-80)*
The most famous living artist in America is Andy Warhol, unfortunately.

John Heilpern, 'The Observer' (1979)

Warhol's art belongs less to the history of painting than to the history of publicity.

Hilton Kramer

The only genius with an IQ of 60.

Gore Vidal

James McNeill Whistler *(1834-1903)*
'Portrait of the Painter's Mother'—This picture has found few admirers and for this result the painter has only to thank himself.

'The (London) Times'

He opened the eyes of the blind and has given great encouragement to the shortsighted.

Oscar Wilde

3
LITERATURE

CRITICISM AND DEFINITIONS

The one thing I most emphatically do not ask of a critic
is that he tells me what I ought to approve or condemn.
I have no objection to his telling me what works and
authors he likes and dislikes.

> *W. H. Auden,*
> *'The Dyer's Hand' (1962)*

One cannot attack a bad book without showing off.

> *W. H. Auden,*
> *'The Dyer's Hand' (1962)*

Some books are to be tasted, others to be swallowed,
and some few to be chewed and digested.

> *Francis Bacon*

The reason why so few good books are written is that so few people who write know anything.

Walter Bagehot

There is nothing like a good negative review to sell a book.

Hugh Barbour

Literature is the question minus the answer.

Roland Barthes (1978)

Friendly attacks should begin with faint praise, but be careful not to use adjectives or phrases of which the publisher can make use in advertisements.

John Betjeman

About the most originality that any writer can hope to achieve honestly is to steal with good judgment.

Josh Billings

A bestseller was a book which somehow sold well simply because it was selling well.

Daniel J. Boorstin

'Tis pleasant, sure, to see one's name in print;
A book's a book although there's nothing in 't.

Lord Byron

A novel is never anything but a philosophy put into images.

Albert Camus

The author who invents a title well
Will always find his covered dullness sell.

Thomas Chatterton

A literary critic is a person who can find a meaning in literature that the author didn't know was there.

'Cleveland Times'

If writers were good businessmen, they'd have too much sense to be writers.

Irvin S. Cobb

The greatest masterpiece in literature is only a dictionary out of order.

Jean Cocteau

A man may as well expect to grow stronger by always eating as wiser by always reading.

Jeremy Collier

In America only the successful writer is important, in France all writers are important, in England no writer is important, and in Australia you have to explain what a writer is.

Geoffrey Cottrell,
'New York Journal' (1961)

When I want to read a book I write one.

Benjamin Disraeli

A critic is at best a waiter at the great table of literature.

Louis Dudek

The chap who said that truth is stranger than fiction died before fiction reached its present state of development.

'Elmira Star Gazette'

People do not deserve to have good writing, they are so pleased with bad.

Ralph Waldo Emerson

There's one good kind of writer—a dead one.

James T. Farrell

A writer is congenitally unable to tell the truth and that is why we call what he writes fiction.

William Faulkner

An author ought to write for the youth of his own generation, the critics of the next, and the schoolmasters of ever afterwards.

F. Scott Fitzgerald

One always tends to overpraise a long book because one has got through it.

E. M. Forster

The paperback is very interesting but I find it will never replace a hardcover book—it makes a very poor doorstop.

Alfred Hitchcock

There is a type of critic whose attitude suggests that the book he is reviewing was written by his kind permission and that the author has grossly abused the privilege.

Lambert Jeffries

The novelist, afraid his ideas may be foolish, slyly puts them in the mouth of some other fool and reserves the right to disavow them.

Diane Johnson, 'New York Times Book Review' (1979)

Authors are easy enough to get on with—if you are fond of children.

Michael Joseph, 'The Observer' (1949)

One man is as good as another until he has written a book.

Benjamin Jowett

Confronted by an absolutely infuriating review it is sometimes helpful for the victim to do a little personal research on the critic. Is there any truth to the rumor that he had no formal education beyond the age of eleven? In any event, is he able to construct a simple English sentence? Do his participles dangle? When moved to lyricism, does he write, "I had a fun time"? Was he ever arrested for burglary? I don't know that you will prove anything this way but it is perfectly harmless and quite soothing.

Jean Kerr

A publisher who writes is like a cow in a milkbar.

Arthur Koestler

Books are a load of crap.

*Philip Larkin, 'A Study
of Reading Habits'*

Having been unpopular in high school is not just cause for book publications.

Fran Lebowitz

It's a crazy business, anyway, writing; locking yourself in a room and inventing conversations is no way for a grown-up to behave. Then, your book is published, the sun comes up as usual, and the world is in no way altered, and it must be someone's fault.

*John Leonard,
'Esquire' (1975)*

It does no harm to repeat as often as you can: "Without me the literary industry would not exist: the publishers, the agents, the subagents, the sub-subagents, the accountants, the libel lawyers, the departments of literature, the professors, the theses, the books of criticism, the reviewers, the book pages—all this vast and proliferating edifice is because of this small, patronized, put-down and underpaid person."

Doris Lessing

One of the greatest creations of the human mind is the art of reviewing books without having read them.

G. C. Lichtenburg

Literature is mostly about having sex, and not much about having babies; life is the other way round.

David Lodge

If you want to get rich from writing, write the sort of thing that's read by persons who move their lips when they're reading to themselves.

Don Marquis

Only a mediocre writer is always at his best.

W. Somerset Maugham

There are no dull subjects. There are only dull writers.

H. L. Mencken

A person who publishes a book willfully appears before the populace with his pants down. If it is a good book nothing can hurt him. If it is a bad book, nothing can help him.

Edna St. Vincent Millay

A man with a belly full of classics is an enemy of the human race.

> *Henry Miller, 'Tropic of Cancer' (1930)*

An optimist is one who believes everything he reads on the jacket of a new book.

> *'Milwaukee Journal'*

First you're an unknown, then you write a book and you move up to obscurity.

> *Martin Myers*

Everywhere I go I'm asked if I think the university stifles writers. My opinion is that they don't stifle enough of them. There's many a bestseller that could have been prevented by a good teacher.

> *Flannery O'Connor*

On her last "Constant Reader" column—I am about to leave literature flat on its face. I don't want to review books any more. It cuts in too much on my reading.

> *Dorothy Parker, 'The New Yorker'*

A work in which there are theories is like an object which still has the ticket that shows its price.

> *Marcel Proust*

The balance sheets of our great publishing houses would not be materially affected if they ceased from tomorrow the publication of poetry and literary criticisms, and most publishers would rejoice to be relieved of the unprofitable burden of vain solicitations which such publication encourages.

Herbert Read

When a new book is published, read an old one.

Samuel Rogers

The road to hell is paved with works-in-progress.

Philip Roth

I hate books; they teach us only to talk about what we do not know.

Jean-Jacques Rousseau

The critics will say as always that literature is decaying. From the time of the first critic up to now they have said nothing else.

Sir Osbert Sitwell

The writer is either a practicing recluse or a delinquent, guilt-ridden one, or both. Usually both.

Susan Sontag

Perversity is the muse of modern literature.

Susan Sontag

Those big-shot writers could never dig the fact that there are more salted peanuts consumed than caviar.

Mickey Spillane

Writers are a little below clowns and a little above trained seals.

John Steinbeck

Satire lies about literary men while they live, and eulogy lies about them when they die.

Voltaire

The 'Literary Digest' says that books have a curative power. Yes: there are some which cure insomnia.

'Washington Post'

Professional reviewers read so many bad books in the course of duty that they get an unhealthy craving for arresting phrases.

Evelyn Waugh

I was never allowed to read the popular American children's books of my day because, as my mother said, the children spoke bad English without the the author's knowing it.

Edith Wharton

If we should ever inaugurate a hall of fame, it would be reserved exclusively and hopefully for authors who, having written four bestsellers, still refrained from starting out on a lecture tour.

E. B. White

I'm never disappointed in literary men. I think they're perfectly charming. It's their works I find so disappointing.

Oscar Wilde

The difference between journalism and literature is that journalism is unreadable and literature is not read.

Oscar Wilde

Nothing induces me to read a novel except when I have to make money by writing about it. I detest them.

Virginia Woolf

WRITERS

Horatio Alger   *(1834-99)*
Horatio Alger wrote the same novel 135 times and never lost his audience.
George Jurgens

Nelson Algren   *(1909-81)*
'A Walk on the Wild Side'—My, how this boy needs editing.
'San Francisco Chronicle'
(1956)

Jane Austen   *(1775-1817)*
Aunt Jane for various circumstances was not so refined as she ought to have been for her talent.

Anonymous Niece

She was the prettiest, silliest, most affected, husband-hunting butterfly ever.
Mary Mitford

Edgar Allan Poe's prose is unreadable—like Jane Austen's. No, there is a difference. I could read his prose on a salary, but not Jane's.

Mark Twain

Francis Bacon   *(1561–1626)*
Lord Bacon could as easily have created the planets as
he could have written *Hamlet.*

Thomas Carlyle

Honoré de Balzac   *(1799–1830)*
A fat little flabby person with the face of a baker, the
clothes of a cobbler, the size of a barrelmaker, the
manners of a stocking salesman, and the dress of an
innkeeper.

Victor de Balabin,
'Diary' (1843)

Ann Beattie   *(b 1947)*
'Love Always'—Beattie's admirable eye for telling de-
tail has unfortunately developed a squint.

'Commonweal' (1985)

Saul Bellow   *(b 1915)*
'The Adventures of Augie March'—All of Those Words,
in denominations of from three to five letters, are
present.

'Library Journal' (1953)

Charlotte Brontë   *(1816–55)*
'Jane Eyre'—I wish her characters would talk a little
less like the heroes and heroines of police reports.

George Eliot

'*Jane Eyre*'—Trivial personalities decomposing in the eternity of print.

Virginia Woolf, 'The Common Reader'

Emily Brontë *(1818-48)*
'*Wuthering Heights*'—All the faults of 'Jane Eyre' are magnified a thousand fold, and the only consolation which we have in reflecting upon it is that it will never be generally read.

James Lorimer, 'North British Review' (1849)

Truman Capote *(1924-84)*
At his worst Capote has less to say than any good writer I know.

Norman Mailer (1959)

On seeing Capote for the first time—For God's sake! What is that?

Harold Ross (1945)

Truman Capote has made lying an art. A minor art.

Gore Vidal

Capote should be heard, not read.

Gore Vidal

I always said Little Truman had a voice so high it could only be detected by a bat.

Tennessee Williams

Lewis Carroll *(1832-98)*
'*Alice's Adventures in Wonderland*'—We fancy that any real child might be more puzzled than enchanted by this stiff, overwrought story.

'*Children's Books*' *(1865)*

Joseph Conrad *(1857-1924)*
Conrad spent a day finding the *mot juste*, and then killed it.

Ford Madox Ford

We could pardon his cheerless themes were it not for the imperturbable solemnity with which he piles the unnecessary on the commonplace.

'*Literature*' *(1898)*

Quentin Crisp [Dennis Pratt] *(b 1908)*
If Quentin Crisp had never existed it is unlikely that anyone would have had the nerve to invent him.

'*The (London) Times*' *(1977)*

Charles Dickens *(1812-70)*
Of Dickens's style it is impossible to speak in praise. It is jerky, ungrammatical, and created by himself in defiance of rules . . . No young novelist should ever dare to imitate the style of Dickens.

Anthony Trollope,
'Autobiography'

Fyodor Dostoyevski *(1821-81)*
They are great parables, the novels, but false art. They are only parables. All the people are fallen angels—even the dirtiest scrubs. This I cannot stomach. People are not fallen angels; they are merely people.

D. H. Lawrence (1916)

George Eliot [Mary Ann Evans] *(1819-80)*
'Adam Bede'—I found out in the first two pages that it was a woman's writing—she supposed that in making a door, you last of all put in the panels!

Thomas Carlyle

William Faulkner *(1897-1962)*
He uses a lot of big words, and his sentences are from here back to the airport.

Carolyn Chute,
'New York Times'

Even those who call Mr. Faulkner our greatest literary sadist do not fully appreciate him, for it is not merely his characters who have to run the gauntlet but also his readers.

Clifton Fadiman,
'The New Yorker' (1934)

F. Scott Fitzgerald   *(1896–1940)*

Fitzgerald never got rid of anything; the ghosts of his adolescence, the failures of his youth, the doubts of his maturity plagued him to the end. He was supremely a part of the world he described, so much a part that he made himself its king and then, when he saw it begin to crumble, he crumbled with it and led it to death.

John Aldridge

Mr. Fitzgerald—I believe that is how he spells his name—seems to believe that plagiarism begins at home.

Zelda Fitzgerald

Gustave Flaubert   *(1821–80)*

You love to diagnose and prescribe for your characters who are obviously your patients. And like every good physician you end in putting all of them to death.

Honoré de Balzac

Ford Madox Ford   *(1873–1939)*
An animated adenoid.

                    Anonymous

His mind was like a Roquefort cheese, so ripe that it was palpably falling to pieces.

                    Van Wyck Brooks

E. M. Forster   *(1879–1970)*
'*Howards End*'—If I were asked to point to a passage which combined all that prose fiction should not be—lurid sentimentality, preposterous morals, turgid and sticky style—I do not think I could point to anything worse than the closing chapters of 'Howards End.' And I am now going to read a few chapters of Mrs. Gaskell to take the taste of 'Howards End' out of my mouth.

                    Edmund Gosse

E. M. Forster never gets any further than warming the teapot. He's a rare fine hand at that. Feel this teapot. Is it not beautifully warm? Yes, but there ain't going to be no tea.

                    Katherine Mansfield

Edward Gibbon   *(1737–94)*
Gibbon's style is detestable; but it is not the worst thing about him.

                    Samuel Taylor Coleridge,
                    'Complete Works' (1853)

Gibbon lived out most of his sex life in his footnotes.

Philip Guedella

Andrew Greeley   *(b 1928)*
'*The Cardinal Sins*'—Enough to give trash a bad name.

'Chicago Sun-Times'
(1982)

Barbara Grizzuti Harrison   *(b 1934)*
'*Foreign Bodies*'—Aphorisms are bad for teeth. They stick in the reader's throat.
Anatole Broyard (1984)

Bret Harte   *(1836-1902)*
Harte, in a mild and colorless way, was that kind of man—that is to say, he was a man without a country; no, not a man—man is too strong a term; he was an invertebrate without a country.

Mark Twain

Nathaniel Hawthorne   *(1804-64)*
There never surely was a powerful, active, continually effective mind less round, more lopsided, than that of Nathaniel Hawthorne.
Anthony Trollope

He never seemed to be doing anything, and yet he did not like to be disturbed at it.

John Greenleaf Whittier

Joseph Heller   *(b 1923)*
'*Catch 22*'—Heller wallows in his own laughter and finally drowns in it. What remains is a debris of sour jokes, stage anger, dirty words, synthetic looniness, and the sort of antic behavior the children fall into when they know they are losing our attention.

Whitney Balliett, 'The New York Times' (1961)

Lillian Hellman   *(1907–84)*
Hellman's memoirs—Every word she writes is a lie, including "and" and "the."
Mary McCarthy (1979)

Ernest Hemingway   *(1898–1961)*
It is of course a commonplace that Hemingway lacks the serene confidence that he is a full-sized man.

Max Eastman, 'The New Republic' (1933)

A literary style of wearing false hair on the chest.

Max Eastman

Always willing to lend a helping hand to the one above him.

F. Scott Fitzgerald

When his cock wouldn't stand up he blew his head off. He sold himself a line of bullshit and he bought it.

Germaine Greer

Hemingway was a jerk.

Harold Robbins

Remarks are not literature.

Gertrude Stein

To her dog—Play, Hemingway, be fierce.

Gertrude Stein

Aldous Huxley   *(1894–1963)*
The stupid person's idea of the clever person.

Elizabeth Bowen,
'The Spectator' (1936)

You could tell by his conversation which volume of the 'Encyclopaedia Britannica' he'd been reading. One day it would be Alps, Andes, and Apennines, and the next it would be the Himalayas and the Hippocratic Oath.

Bertrand Russell (1965)

Henry James   *(1843–1916)*
It's not that he "bites off more than he can chew" but he chews more than he bites off.

Clover Adams

Henry James had a mind so fine that no idea could violate it.

T. S. Eliot

An idiot, and a Boston idiot, to boot, than which there is nothing lower in the world.

H. L. Mencken,
'The American Scene'

The Bostonians—And as for 'The Bostonians,' I would rather be damned to John Bunyan's heaven than read that.

Mark Twain (1885)

Mr. Henry James writes fiction as if it were a painful duty.

Oscar Wilde

James Joyce   *(1882-1941)*
'Ulysses'—Written by a man with a diseased mind and soul so black that he would even obscure the darkness of hell.

Anonymous U.S. Senator

On his letters—An account of some of these acts makes Henry Miller's crudest imaginations seem as chaste as a nun's diary.

James Atlas

The key to reading 'Ulysses' . . . so much of it consists of rather lengthy demonstrations of how a novel ought not to be written.

Aldous Huxley,
'Paris Review'

Why don't you write books people can read?

Nora Joyce

James Joyce's ultimate works are like a man who is too shy to write a love letter except in the form of a crossword puzzle.

Constant Lambert,
'Music Ho!'

In Ireland they try to make a cat clean by rubbing its nose in its own filth. Mr. Joyce has tried the same treatment on the human subject.

George Bernard Shaw

Jack Kerouac *(1922-69)*
'*On the Road*'—That's not writing, that's typing.

Truman Capote

D. H. Lawrence *(1885-1930)*
'*Lady Chatterley's Lover*'—Mr. Lawrence has a diseased mind. He is obsessed by sex and we have no doubt that he will be ostracized by all except the most degenerate coteries in the world.

John Bull (1928)

'*Lady Chatterley's Lover*'—The pictorial account of the day-to-day life of an English gamekeeper is full of considerable interest to outdoor readers. Unfortunately, one is obliged to wade through many pages of extraneous material. In this reviewer's opinion, the book cannot take the place of J. R. Miller's 'Practical Gamekeeping.'

'Field and Stream'

I ask you, is anything in life or literature past or present in earth, heaven or hell, anything more devastatingly tedious than D.H.L.'s interest in the human genitalia?

G. W. Lyttelton

T. E. Lawrence [of Arabia] *(1888–1935)*
Arabian Lawrence, who whatever his claims as a man, was surely a sonorous fake as a writer.

Kingsley Amis

Jack London *(1876–1916)*
Like Peter Pan, he never grew up, and he lived his own stories with such intensity that he ended by believing them himself.

Ford Madox Ford

Herman Melville *(1819–91)*
'*Moby-Dick, or The Whale*'—A huge dose of hyperbolical slang, maudlin sentimentalism, and tragi-comic bubble-and-squeak.

William H. Ainsworth,
'*New Monthly Magazine*'

His vocabulary was large, fluent, eloquent, but it was excessive, inaccurate, and unliterary. He wrote too easily, and at too great length, his pen sometimes running away from him, and from his readers.

Richard Stoddard

George Meredith   *(1828–1909)*
His style is chaos illumined by flashes of lightning. As
a writer he has mastered everything except language.
As a novelist he can do everything except tell a story.
As an artist he is everything except articulate.

> *Oscar Wilde, 'The Decay
> of Living' (1889)*

Henry Miller   *(1891–1980)*
He is not really a writer, but a nonstop talker to whom
someone has given a typewriter.

> *Gerald Brenan, 'Thought
> in a Dry Season'*

'Tropic of Capricorn'—A gadfly with delusions of
grandeur.
> *'Time' (1962)*

John O'Hara   *(1905–70)*
'Sermons and Soda-Water'—O'Hara normally puts
everything into a novel, including the kitchen sink
complete with stopped drain, plumber, and plumber's
mate, and does this not once but four or five times per
book. The novella form has merely limited the author
in a statistical way; one kitchen sink is all he can fit
into his predetermined space.

> *'Atlantic Monthly' (1960)*

Hard to lay down, but easy not to pick up.

Malcolm Cowley

S. J. Perelman   *(1904-70)*
Before they made S. J. Perelman they broke the mold.

Anonymous

Edgar Allan Poe   *(1809-49)*
An unmanly sort of man whose love life seems to have been largely confined to crying in laps and playing mouse.

W. H. Auden

Marcel Proust   *(1871-1922)*
Letter of rejection for 'Remembrance of Things Past'—
I may be dead from the neck up, but rack my brains as I may I can't see why a chap should need thirty pages to describe how he turns over in bed before going to sleep.

Marc Humbolt (1912)

I was reading Proust for the first time. Very poor stuff. I think he was mentally defective.

Evelyn Waugh (1948)

Philip Roth   *(b 1933)*
'Portnoy's Complaint'—Philip Roth is a good writer,
but I wouldn't want to shake hands with him.

Jacqueline Susann

Jean Rhys   *(1894–1979)*
Her novels read now like a single continuing work with
the same heroine and the same single, persistent, dis-
connected disaster of a life in which only four things
can be relied on: loneliness, fear, booze, and lack of
money.

A. Alvarez,
'The Observer' (1979)

Carl Sandburg   *(1878–1967)*
He is submerged in adolescence. Give Sandburg a
mind, and you perhaps destroy him.

Sherwood Anderson
(1919)

'Lincoln'—The cruelest thing that has happened to
Lincoln since he was shot by Booth has been to fall
into the hands of Carl Sandburg.

Edmund Wilson,
'Time'

Dorothy L. Sayers   *(1893–1957)*
Her slickness in writing has blinded many readers to
the fact that her stories, considered as detective stories,
are very bad ones. They lack the minimum of probabil-
ity that even a detective story ought to have, and the
crime is always committed in a way that is incredibly
tortuous and quite uninteresting.

*George Orwell, 'New
English Review' (1936)*

Hubert Selby   *(b 1929)*
'Last Exit to Brooklyn'—This is Grove Press's extra
special dirty book for fall.
                                 'Time' (1965)

Alexander Solzhenitsyn   *(b 1918)*
He is a bad novelist and a fool. The combination usually makes for great popularity in the U.S.

Gore Vidal (1980)

Arianna Stassinopoulos   *(b 1950)*
So boring you fall asleep halfway through her name.

*Alan Bennett,
The Observer (1983)*

John Steinbeck   *(1902-68)*
After a dozen books Steinbeck still looks like a distinguished apprentice, and what is so striking in his work is its inconclusiveness, his moving approach to human life and yet his failure to be creative with it.

Alfred Kazin

Jacqueline Susann   *(1926-74)*
'Valley of the Dolls'—For the reader who has put away comic books but isn't ready for editorials in the 'Daily News'.

Gloria Steinem,
'New York Times' (1976)

James Thurber   *(1894-1961)*
A tall, thin, spectacled man with the face of a harassed rat.

Russell Maloney,
'Saturday Review'

Alice B. Toklas   *(1877-1967)*
Miss Toklas was incredibly ugly, uglier than almost anyone I had ever met. A thin, withered creature, she sat hunched in her chair, in her heavy tweed suit and her thick lisle stockings, impregnable and indifferent. She had a huge nose, a dark moustache, and her dark-dyed hair was combed into absurd bangs over her forehead.

Otto Friedrich,
'Esquire' (1968)

J. R. R. Tolkien   *(1892–1975)*
He talks in shorthand and then smudges it.

Anonymous

His was not a true imagination. He made it all up.

H. V. Dyson

Leo Tolstoy   *(1828–1910)*
'War and Peace'—I took a speed reading course and
read 'War and Peace' in twenty minutes. It involves
Russia.

Woody Allen

Diana Trilling   *(b 1905)*
'The Death of the Scarsdale Diet Doctor'—If you are
unhealthily addicted to reading about murder trials,
this book may cure you.

*John Carey, 'The Sunday
(London) Times' (1982)*

Mark Twain   *(1835–1910)*
'Huckleberry Finn'—If Mr. Clemens cannot think of
something better to tell our pure-minded lads and
lasses, he had better stop writing for them.

Louisa May Alcott (1885)

A hack writer who would not have been considered fourth rate in Europe, who tried out a few of the old proven "sure-fire" literary skeletons with sufficient local color to intrigue the superficial and the lazy.

William Faulkner

Gore Vidal *(b 1925)*
'*Lincoln*'—He offers the never-never land of convenient clichés.

Paul Gray, 'Time' (1984)

'*Two Sisters*'—He seems to have gone to his icebox, pulled out all the cold obsessions, mixed them in a bowl, beat too lightly and baked too long . . . Aspiring to a soufflé, he achieves a pancake at which the reader saws without much attention . . . There are too many ironies in the fire.

John Leonard,
'New York Times' (1970)

Kurt Vonnegut *(b 1922)*
'*Breakfast of Champions*'—From time to time it's nice to have a book you can hate—it clears the pipes—and I hate this book.

Peter Prescott,
'Newsweek' (1973)

Horace Walpole *(1717–97)*
The conformation of his mind was such that whatever was little seemed to him great, and whatever was great seemed to him little.

       Thomas Macaulay

Evelyn Waugh *(1903–66)*
Mr. Waugh, I always feel, is an antique in search of a period, a snob in search of a class, perhaps even a mystic in search of a beatific vision.

       Malcolm Muggeridge,
       'The Most of . . .'

Noah Webster *(1758–1843)*
In conversation he is even duller than in writing, if that is possible.

       Juliana Smith

Rebecca West *(1892–1983)*
Rebecca was a busy liar in her distinguished old age, reinventing her past for gullible biographers.

       Walter Clemons,
       'Newsweek' (1984)

She writes like a loom, producing her broad rich fabric with hardly a thought of how it will make up into a shape.

       H. G. Wells

Edith Wharton   *(1862–1937)*
The glittering structure of her cultivation sits on her novels like a rather showy icing that detracts from the cake beneath.

Louis Auchinloss (1965)

P. G. Wodehouse   *(1881–1975)*
Literature's performing flea.

Sean O'Casey

Thomas Wolfe   *(1900–38)*
If it must be Thomas, let it be Mann, and if it must be Wolfe let it be Nero, but let it never be Thomas Wolfe.

Peter De Vries

Thomas Wolfe has always seemed to be the most over-rated, long-winded and boring of reputable American novelists.

Edith Oliver

Virginia Woolf   *(1882–1941)*
In real estate parlance—a single room.

Anonymous

Replying to the author's dislike of his drawing of her—Mrs. Woolf's complaint should be addressed to her creator, who made her, rather than me.

Sir Cecil Beaton

POETRY

A poet is someone who is astonished by everything.

Anonymous

Poetry is living proof that rhyme doesn't pay.

Anonymous

Verse is a special illness of the ear.

W. H. Auden

I gave up on new poetry myself thirty years ago, when most of it began to read like coded messages passing between lonely aliens in a hostile world.

Russell Baker (1986)

Anticipating that most poetry will be worse than carrying heavy luggage through O'Hare Airport, the public reads very little of it.

Russell Baker (1986)

Elegy—a composition in verse, in which, without employing any of the methods of humor, the writer aims to produce in the reader's mind the dampest kind of dejection. The most famous English example begins somewhat like this:

> The cur foretells this knell of parting day;
> The loafing herd winds slowly o'er the lea
> The wise man homeward plods; I only stay
> To fiddle-faddle in a minor key.

Ambrose Bierce

I know that poetry is indispensable, but to what I could not say.

Jean Cocteau (1955)

A poet is a liar who always speaks the truth.

Jean Cocteau

Some prose writers go from bad to verse.

'Columbia Record'

Idleness, that is the curse of other men, is the nurse of poets.

D'Arcy Cresswell

Poetry is what happens when an anxiety meets a technique.

Lawrence Durrell

A poet in history is divine; but a poet in the next room is a joke.

Max Eastman

In the case of many poets, the most important thing for them to do is to write as little as possible.

T. S. Eliot

The immature poet imitates; the mature poet plagiarizes.

T. S. Eliot

Poetry is what gets lost in translation.

Robert Frost

A true sonnet goes eight lines and then takes a turn for the better or worse and goes six or eight lines more.

Robert Frost

There is no money in poetry; but then there is no poetry in money, either.

Robert Graves

I could no more define poetry than a terrier can define a rat.

A. E. Housman

I never knowed a successful man who could quote poetry.

Kin Hubbard

The world, we believe, is pretty well agreed in thinking that the shorter a prize poem is, the better.

Thomas Macaulay

Poetry is the language of a state of crisis.

Stéphane Mallarmé

Publishing a volume of verse is like dropping a rose petal down the Grand Canyon and waiting for the echo.

Don Marquis,
'The Sun Dial'

I'd rather be a great bad poet than a good bad poet.

Ogden Nash

A publisher of today would as soon see a burglar in his office as a poet.

Henry de Vere Stacpoole

All bad poetry springs from genuine feeling.

Oscar Wilde (1890)

POETS

On an anonymous couplet—Excellent were it not for its length.

Sebastian Chamfort

Rejection slip returned with a poem entitled "Why Do I Live?"—Because you send your poem by mail.

Eugene Field

On an anonymous couplet—Very nice, though there are dull stretches.

Antoine de Rivarol

Matthew Arnold   *(1822-88)*
Poor Matt, he's gone to Heaven, no doubt—but he won't like God.

Robert Louis Stevenson

W. H. Auden   *(1907-73)*
My face looks like a wedding cake that has been left out in the rain.

W. H. Auden

One never steps twice into the same Auden.

Randall Jarrell, 'The Third Book of Criticism' (1969)

An engaging, bookish, American talent, too verbose to be memorable and too intellectual to be moving.

Philip Larkin

Lord Byron   *(1788-1824)*
On Byron's death—The world is rid of Lord Byron, but the deadly slime of his touch remains.

John Constable

The most vulgar-minded genius that ever produced a great effect in literature.

George Eliot

Chang Tzu
Chang Tzu was born in the fourth century before Christ. The publication of this book in English, two thousand years after his death, is obviously premature.

Anonymous

Geoffrey Chaucer   *(1340-1400)*
Mr. C. had talent, but he couldn't spel. No man has a right to be a lit'rary man onless he knows how to spel. It is a pity that Chawcer, who had geneyus, was so unedicated. He's the wus speller I know of.

> *Artemus Ward,*
> *'Chaucer's Poems'*

Samuel Taylor Coleridge   *(1772-1834)*
"Ancient Mariner"—A man who would not have taken so well if he had been called the Old Sailor.

> *Samuel Butler*

Never did I see such apparatus get ready for thinking, and so little thought. He mounts scaffolding, pulleys, and tackles, gathers all the tools in the neighborhood with labor, with noise, demonstration, precept, and sets—three bricks.

> *Thomas Carlyle*

E. E. Cummings   *(1894-1962)*
He replaces the old poetic conventions with equally limited conventions of his own.

> *Allen Tate*

Dante *(1265-1321)*
A hyena that wrote poetry in tombs.

Friedrich Nietzsche

Emily Dickinson *(1830-86)*
An eccentric, dreamy, half-educated recluse in an out-of-the-way New England village (or anywhere else) cannot with impunity set at defiance the laws of gravitation and grammar.

Thomas B. Aldrich

John Dryden *(1631-1700)*
"The Spanish Friar"—This litter of epithets make the poem look like a bitch overstocked with puppies, and sucks the sense almost to skin and bone.

Jeremy Collier (1698)

His imagination resembles the wings of an ostrich. It enabled him to run, though not to soar.

*Thomas Macaulay,
'Essays'*

William Dunbar *(1465-1530)*
Dunbar writes so scathingly of women that, when he treats them in complimentary vein, doubts have been cast upon his authorship.

J. W. Baxter, 'Dunbar'

T. S. Eliot   *(1888-1965)*
T. S. Eliot is quite at a loss
When clubwomen bustle across
At literary teas
Crying, "What, if you please,
Did you mean by 'The Mill on the Floss'?"

W. H. Auden

Ralph Waldo Emerson   *(1803-82)*
Like most poets, preachers, and metaphysicians, he burst into conclusions at a spark of evidence.

Henry Seidel Canby,
'Classical Americans'

That everlasting rejector of all that is, and seeker for he knows not what.

Nathaniel Hawthorne

I could readily see in Emerson a gaping flaw. It was the insinuation that had he lived in those days when the world was made, he might have offered some valuable suggestions.

Herman Melville

Robert Frost   *(1874-1963)*
If it were thought that anything I wrote was influenced by Robert Frost I would take that particular piece of mine, shred it, and flush it down the toilet, hoping not to clog the pipes.

James Dickey

Allen Ginsberg *(b 1926)*

"Howl"—It is only fair to Allen Ginsberg to remark on the utter lack of decorum of any kind in this dreadful little volume. "Howl" is meant to be a noun, but I can't help taking it as an imperative.

> *John Hollander,*
> *'Partisan Review' (1956)*

Oliver Goldsmith *(1728–74)*

Poor fellow! He hardly knew an ass from a mule, nor a turkey from a goose but when he saw it on the table.

> *Richard Cumberland*

Thomas Gray *(1716–71)*

Thomas Gray walks as if he had fouled his small-clothes and looks as if he smelt it.
> *Christopher Smart*

Ted Hughes *(b 1930)*

Ted Hughes has been appointed Poet Laureate to succeed Sir John Betjeman, which is a bit like appointing a grim young crow to replace a cuddly old teddy bear.

> *Philip Howard, 'The*
> *(London) Times' (1984)*

John Keats *(1795–1821)*

A tadpole of the Lakes.

> *Lord Byron,*
> *'Journal' (1820)*

Such writing is a sort of mental masturbation—he is always frigging his imagination. I don't mean he is indecent, but viciously soliciting his own ideas into a state, which is neither poetry nor anything else but a Bedlam produced by raw pork and opium.

Lord Byron (1820)

Joyce Kilmer   *(1886-1918)*
"Trees"—One of the most annoying pieces of verse within my knowledge. Surely the Kilmer tongue must not have been very far from the Kilmer cheek when she [sic] wrote, "Poems are made by fools like me."

Heywood Broun

Rudyard Kipling   *(1865-1936)*
Mr. Kipling stands for everything in this cankered world which I would wish were otherwise.

Dylan Thomas

Walter Savage Landor   *(1775-1864)*
Upon the work of Walter Landor
I am unfit to write with candor.
If you can read it, well and good;
But as for me, I never could.   *Dorothy Parker*

Henry Wadsworth Longfellow *(1807-82)*
His didactics are all out of place. He has written brilliant poems, by accident, that is to say, when permitting his genius to get the better of his conventional habit of thinking, a habit deduced from German study.

Edgar Allan Poe

Edna St. Vincent Millay *(1892-1950)*
The career of Edna Millay presented the still sadder spectacle of a poet who withered on the stalk before attaining fruition.

George F. Whicher

John Milton *(1608-74)*
Read not Milton, for he is dry.

C. S. Calverly

'Paradise Lost'—One of those books which the reader admires and lays down and forgets to take up again. Its perusal is a duty rather than a pleasure.

Samuel Johnson

Alexander Pope *(1688-1744)*
He hardly drank tea without a stratagem.

Samuel Johnson

His more ambitious works may be classified as careless thinking carefully versified.

James Russell Lowell

Ezra Pound   *(1885-1972)*
Mr. Pound is humane, but not human.

E. E. Cummings

A village explainer, excellent if you were a village, but if you were not, not.

Gertrude Stein

Carl Sandburg   *(1878-1967)*
The poet lariat of Chicago.

Richard J. Daley (1960)

William Shakespeare   *(1564-1616)*
Never did any author precipitate himself from such heights of thought to so low expressions, as he often does. He is the very Janus of poets; he wears, almost everywhere, two faces: and you have scarce begun to admire the one, e'er you despise the other.

John Dryden

Percy Bysshe Shelley   *(1792-1822)*
A beautiful and ineffectual angel, beating in the void his luminous wings in vain.

Matthew Arnold, 'Essays'

Dame Edith Sitwell *(1887-1964)*
I am fairly unrepentant about her poetry. I really think that three quarters of it is gibberish. However, I must crush down these thoughts, otherwise the dove of peace will shit on me.

Noël Coward,
'Diary' (1962)

In full regalia, she looked like Lyndon B. Johnson dressed up like Elizabeth I.

'Time' (1965)

Gertrude Stein *(1874-1946)*
There's a famous family named Stein—
There's Gert, and there's Ep, and their's Ein;
Gert's poems are bunk,
Ep's statues are junk,
And no one understands Ein.

Anonymous

Gertrude Stein was masterly in making nothing happen very slowly.

Clifton Fadiman,
'Puzzlements'

It's a shame you never knew her before she went to pot. You know a funny thing, she never could write dialogue. It was terrible. She learned how to do it from me.

Ernest Hemingway, 'Green
Hills of Africa' (1935)

Alfred, Lord Tennyson *(1809-92)*
"Maud"—It has one vowel too many in the title, and it makes sense no matter which is deleted.

Anonymous

Dylan Thomas *(1914-53)*
His poems were strewn with wild, organic, telescoped images underneath which, perhaps, ran a submerged stream of poetic thought.
Robert Graves,
'The Long Weekend'

Henry David Thoreau *(1817-62)*
Behind a mask of self-exaltation Thoreau performed as before a mirror—and first of all for his own edification. He was a fragile Narcissus embodied in a homely New Englander.
Leon Edel

The nullifier of Civilization, who insisted on nibbling his asparagus at the wrong end.

Oliver Wendell Holmes, Sr.

Louis Untermeyer *(1885-1977)*
Upon meeting the poet—And you're "Required Reading!"
Anonymous college student

Walt Whitman   *(1819-92)*
'Leaves of Grass'—To call it poetry, in any sense, would be mere abuse of language.

William Allingham (1857)

Oscar Wilde   *(1854-1900)*
Of his poems not one has survived, for he was totally lacking in a poetic voice of his own; what he wrote was an imitation of a poetry-in-general.

W. H. Auden

He festooned the dung heap on which he had placed himself with sonnets as people grow honeysuckle around outdoor privies.

Quentin Crisp

William Wordsworth   *(1770-1850)*
When Wordsworth tries to write according to his theories, the result is nearly always flat.

W. H. Auden

In his youth, Wordsworth sympathized with the French Revolution, went to France, wrote good poetry, and had a natural daughter. At this period, he was a "bad" man. Then he became "good," abandoned his daughter, adopted correct principles, and wrote bad poetry.

Bertrand Russell

4
DRAMA

GENERAL

If Attila the Hun were alive today, he'd be a drama
critic.

Edward Albee

One of the first and most important things for a critic
to learn is how to sleep undetected in the theater.

William Archer

I don't see why people want new plays all the time.
What would happen to concerts if people wanted new
music all the time?

Clive Barnes

I find that when I dislike what I see on the stage that I can be vastly amusing, but when I write about something I like, I find I am appallingly dull.

Max Beerbohm

Critics should be searched for certain adjectives at the door of the theatre. Irreverent, probing, and (above all) satirical. I would have all such adjectives left with their coats in the foyer, only to be redeemed when their notices are written.

Alan Bennett

A play is like a cigar. If it is a failure no amount of puffing will make it draw. If it is a success everybody wants a box.

Henry F. Bryan

The state of alienation known as Brechtian, but what we used to call "bored stiff."

John Coleman

I don't like propaganda in the theater unless it is disguised so brilliantly that the audience mistakes it for entertainment.

Noël Coward

Asking a working actor what he thinks of critics is like asking a lamppost how it feels about dogs.

Christopher Hampton

Coughing in the theater is not a respiratory ailment. It is a criticism.

Alan Jay Lerner,
'The Street Where I Live'

All playwrights should be dead for three hundred years.

Joseph L. Mankiewicz

A drama critic is a person who surprises the playwright by informing him what he meant.

Wilson Mizner

The drama critic who is without prejudice is on the same plane with the general who does not believe in the taking of life.

George Jean Nathan,
'Comedians All'

Opening night is the night before the play is ready to open.

George Jean Nathan

A drama critic is a man who leaves no turn unstoned.

George Bernard Shaw

Reviewing has one advantage over suicide; in suicide you take it out on yourself; in reviewing you take it out on other people.

George Bernard Shaw

To be able to write a play a man must be sensitive, imaginative, naive, gullible, passionate: he must be something of an imbecile, something of a poet, something of a liar, something of a damn fool.

Robert E. Sherwood

A playwright is a lay preacher peddling the ideas of his time in popular form.

August Strindberg

Show me a congenital eavesdropper with the instincts of a peeping tom and I will show you the makings of a dramatist.

Kenneth Tynan (1957)

The sheer complexity of writing a play always had dazzled me. In an effort to understand it, I became a critic.

Kenneth Tynan,
'New York Mirror' (1963)

By increasing the size of the keyhole, today's playwrights are in danger of doing away with the door.

> *Peter Ustinov, 'Christian Science Monitor' (1962)*

Ideal dramatic criticism is unqualified appreciation.

> *Oscar Wilde*

PLAYWRIGHTS

Anonymous
That poor man. He's completely unspoiled by failure.

> *Noël Coward*

Samuel Beckett   *(1906–89)*
In attempting to depict the boredom of human existence, he has run the very grave risk of thoroughly boring his reader.

> *'San Francisco Chronicle'*

Bertolt Brecht   *(1898–1956)*
I don't regard Brecht as a man of iron-gray purpose and intellect, I think he is a theatrical whore of the first quality.

> *Peter Hall*

Noël Coward *(1899–1973)*

One can't read any of Noël Coward's plays now; they are written in the most topical and perishable way imaginable; the cream in them turns sour overnight.

Cyril Connolly (1937)

Lady Isabella Gregory *(1852–1932)*

Now that the Abbey Players are world-renowned, I begin to realize that with such an audience and such actors an author is hardly needed. Good acting covers a multitude of defects. It explains the success of Lady Gregory's plays.

Oliver St. J. Gogarty

Lillian Hellman *(1907–84)*

'*Toys in the Attic*'—It is curious how incest, impotence, nymphomania, religious mania, and real estate speculation can be so dull.

Richard Findlater,
'*Time and Tide*' *(1961)*

Henrik Ibsen *(1828–1906)*

'*Peer Gynt*'—Written by a mad poet. One goes crazy oneself if reading this book.

Hans Christian Andersen
(1870)

Henry Arthur Jones   *(1851–1929)*
The first rule for a playwright is not to write like Henry
Arthur Jones. The second and third rules are the same.

Oscar Wilde

George S. Kaufman   *(1889–1961)*
He was like a dry cracker. Brittle.

Edna Ferber

Clare Booth Luce   *(1903–1987)*
No woman of our time has gone further with less mental equipment.

Clifton Fadiman

Eugene O'Neill   *(1888–1953)*
Though he possesses the tragic vision, he cannot claim
the tragic tongue.

John Mason Brown

Sir Arthur Pinero   *(1855–1934)*
His eyebrows look like the skins of some small mam-
mal just not large enough to be used as mats.

Max Beerbohm

William Shakespeare   *(1564–1616)*
Shakespeare's name, you may depend on it, stands
absurdly too high and will go down. He had no inven-

tion as to stories, none whatever. He took all his plots from old novels, and threw their stories into a dramatic shape, at as little expense of thought as you or I could turn his plays back again into prose tales.

Lord Byron (1814)

I have tried lately to read Shakespeare, and found it so intolerably dull that it nauseated me.

Charles Darwin

The remarkable thing about Shakespeare is that he really is very good, in spite of all the people who say he is very good.

Robert Graves

Playing Shakespeare is very tiring. You never get to sit down, unless you're a king.

Josephine Hull,
'Time' (1953)

George Bernard Shaw   *(1856–1950)*
I really enjoy only his stage directions; the dialogue is vortical, and I find, fatiguing. It is like being harangued. He uses the English language like a truncheon.

Max Beerbohm

Shaw's works make me admire the magnificent tolerance and broadmindedness of the English.

James Joyce

Shaw writes his plays for the ages, the ages between five and twelve.

George Jean Nathan

Sherard Blaw, the dramatist who had discovered himself, and who had given so ungrudgingly of his discovery to the world.

Saki (H. H. Munro)

Richard Brinsley Sheridan *(1751–1816)*
Every man has his element. Sheridan's is hot water.

John Eldon

Oscar Wilde *(1854–1900)*
From beginning to end Wilde performed his life and continued to do so even after fame had taken the plot out of his hands.

W. H. Auden

Oscar and George Bernard
    Cannot be reconciled.
When I'm Wilde about Shaw
I'm not Shaw about Wilde.

Freddie Oliver

When Oscar came to join his God,
Not earth to earth, but sod to sod,
It was for sinners such as this
    Hell was created bottomless.

Algernon Swinburne

Tennessee Williams   *(1911–83)*

Williams's problem is not a lack of talent. It is, perhaps, an ambiguity of aim; he seems to want to kick the world in the pants and yet be the world's sweetheart, to combine the glories of martyrdom with the comforts of success.

Eric Bentley,
'The New Republic'

If a swamp alligator could talk, it would sound like Tennessee Williams.

Rex Reed (1972)

MUSICALS

Musicals—a series of catastrophes ending with a floor show.

Oscar Levant

Musicals are to the theater what wines are to a substantial dinner.

George Jean Nathan

It seems that the moment anyone gets hold of an exclamation mark these days, he promptly sits down and writes a musical show around it.

George Jean Nathan

Anonymous
I have knocked everything in this play except the chorus girls' knees, and there God anticipated me.

Percy Hammond

I could eat alphabet soup and shit better lyrics!

Johnny Mercer (1975)

It contains a number of tunes one goes into the theater humming.

Kenneth Tynan

'Annie'
I had to hit myself on the head afterward with a small hammer to get that stupid "Tomorrow" song out of my head.

Ian Shoales

'Camelot'

It's like 'Parsifal' without the jokes.

Noël Coward

'Cats'

This spectacle could have been manufactured by Disney World, using audio-animatronics instead of actors; I perceived no sign of flesh-and-blood behavior beneath the glitter and flash.

Robert Brustein

'Flower Drum Song' (1960)

An American musical, so bad that at times I longed for the boy-meets-tractor theme of Soviet drama.

Bernard Levin,
'Daily Express'

Gilbert and Sullivan

One can always count on Gilbert and Sullivan for a rousing finale, full of words and music, signifying nothing.

Tom Lehrer

'Godspell'

'Godspell' is back . . . For those who missed it the first time, this is your golden opportunity: you can miss it again.

Michael Billington, 'The Guardian' (1981)

'Hair'
Why should I pay ten dollars for something I can see in the bathroom for nothing?
Groucho Marx

'Jesus Christ Superstar'
It will flow on, if only at a syrup's pace. Religion and atheism will both survive it.

Stanley Kauffmann

'My Fair Lady'
I must say [George] Bernard Shaw is greatly improved by music.
T. S. Eliot

'Oh! Calcutta'
The sort of show that gives pornography a bad name.
Clive Barnes

The trouble with nude dancing is that not everything stops when the music stops.
Robert Helpman

'Oklahoma!'
No legs, no jokes, no chance. *Michael Todd (1943)*

'Phantom of the Opera'

Mr. [Andrew] Lloyd Webber has again written a score so generic that most of the songs could be reordered and redistributed among the characters (indeed, among other Lloyd Webber musicals) without altering the show's story or meaning.

'New York Times'

'Porgy and Bess'

Falsely conceived and rather clumsily executed . . . crooked folklore and halfway opera.

Virgil Thomson

'Starlight Express'

A confusing jamboree of piercing noise, routine roller-skating, misogyny, and Orwellian special effects, 'Starlight Express' is the perfect gift for the kid who has everything except parents.

'New York Times'

'Take a Bow'

The Murtah Sisters murtahed several songs.

Willela Waldorf,
'New York Post'

DANCE

Dancing is the perpendicular expression of a horizontal desire.

Anonymous

Most ballet teachers in the United States are terrible. If they were in medicine, everyone would be poisoned.

George Balanchine,
'Newsweek' (1964)

Try everything once except incest and folk dancing.

Sir Thomas Beecham

On the cost of ballet tickets—That's a lot to see buggers jump.

Nigel Bruce

Am I supposed to believe that a man prancing about at the Royal Ballet in a pair of tights is part of my heritage?

Terry Dicks

I am the enemy of ballet, which I look upon as false, absurd, and outside the domain of art. I thank God that a cruel destiny did not inflict on me the career of a ballet dancer.

Isadora Duncan,
'My Life' (1928)

Dancers ennoble what is vulgar; but they degrade what is heroic.

Joseph Joubert

Transplanting ballet to the U.S.A. is like trying to raise a palm tree in Dakota.

Lincoln Kirstein

The man who doesn't know which way to turn is probably learning the latest dance.

Bert H. Kruse

I'm a guy who likes to keep score. With ballet I can't tell who's ahead.

Fiorello La Guardia

All those great swans chasing that absurd young man!

Terence Rattigan

The ballet is simply a lewd performance.

Leo Tolstoy

Fred Astaire *(1899–1987)*
Can't act. Slightly bald. Can dance a little.

Anonymous screen test

Watching the nondancing, nonsinging Astaire is like watching a grounded skylark.

Vincent Canby

Isadora Duncan   *(1878–1927)*
On her performance—Made me think of Grant's Tomb in love.

Finley Peter Dunne

A woman whose face looked as if it had been made out of sugar and someone had licked it.

George Bernard Shaw

Martha Graham   *(1894–1991)*
I'm afraid she is going to give birth to a cube.

Stark Young

Rudolf Nureyev   *(1938–93)*
During one modern ballet . . . Nureyev and a drowsily sexy ballerina engaged in a long attempt to pull each other's tights off without using fingers, toes, or teeth. It sounds difficult, but was fun to watch, although probably not as much fun as it was to do.

Clive James,
'The Observer' (1980)

5
FILM

GENERAL

The criterion for judging whether a picture is successful or not is time.

Peter Bogdanovich

On movie moguls—They were monsters and pirates and bastards right down to the bottom of their feet but they loved the movies. Some of the jerks running the business today don't even have faces.

Richard Brooks (1970)

I would take a bad script and a good director any day against a good script and a bad director.

Bette Davis

Filmmaking has now reached the same stage as sex—it's all technique and no feeling.

Penelope Gilliatt

Cinema is the most beautiful fraud in the world.

Jean-Luc Godard

Movies are just another form of merchandising—we have our factory, which is called a stage; we make a product, we color it, we title it, and we ship it out in cans.

Cary Grant

A movie is never any better than the stupidest man connected with it.

Ben Hecht

The movies are an eruption of trash that has tamed the American mind and retarded the Americans from being cultured people.

Ben Hecht

Film is not an art of scholars but of illiterates.

Werner Herzog

An epic is the easiest kind of picture to make badly.

Charlton Heston

The length of a film should be directly related to the endurance of the human bladder.

Alfred Hitchcock

Critics have never been able to discover a unifying theme in my films. For that matter, neither have I.

John Huston

On colorization of black-and-white films—It's not color; it's like pouring forty tablespoons of sugary water over a roast.

John Huston (1986)

My reaction to porno films is as follows: After the first ten minutes, I want to go home and screw. After the first twenty minutes, I never want to screw again as long as I live.

Erica Jong

The words "Kiss Kiss Bang Bang," which I saw on an Italian movie poster, are perhaps the briefest statement imaginable of the basic appeal of the movies.

Pauline Kael (1968)

I wouldn't take the advice of a lot of critics on how to shoot a close-up of a teapot.

David Lean

You can fool all the people all the time if the advertising is right and the budget is big enough.

Joseph E. Levine

Damn it! Can't they realize that most moviegoers are sick to death of the dingy sexpot who lives next door and the hairy oaf who's screwing her?

Ray Milland

A double feature is a show that enables you to sit through a picture you don't care to see, so you can see one you don't like.

Henry Morgan

Those who can't—teach. And those who can't do either—review.

Burt Reynolds

This isn't exactly a stable business. It's like trying to stand up in a canoe with your pants down.

Cliff Robertson

There is only one thing that can kill the movies—and that is education.

Will Rogers,
'Autobiography'

Some films could only have been cast in one way: screen tests were given and the losers got the parts.

Gene Shalit (1971)

I love films, but the film business is shit.

Oliver Stone

HOLLYWOOD

Malice in Wonderland.

Anonymous

Siberia with palms.

Anonymous

Paradise with a lobotomy.

Anonymous

Where the average actor has more lines in his face than in his script.

Anonymous

There is nothing wrong with Hollywood that six first-class funerals wouldn't solve.

Anonymous

In Hollywood you can be forgotten while you're out of the room going to the toilet.

Anonymous

A Hollywood marriage is one in which the couple vow to be faithful until after the honeymoon.

Anonymous

This is a back-stabbing, scum-sucking, small-minded town.

Roseanne Arnold,
'Hollywood Reporter'
(1990)

What I like about Hollywood is that one can get along by knowing two words of English—swell and lousy.

Vicki Baum

Hollywood is full of genius. And all it lacks is talent.

Henri Bernstein

I came out here with one suit and everybody said I looked like a bum. Twenty years later Marlon Brando came out with only a sweatshirt and the town drooled over him. That shows how much Hollywood has progressed.

Humphrey Bogart

On being asked to describe Hollywood—Can a fish describe the murky water in which it swims?

Albert Einstein

I can match bottoms with anyone in Hollywood.

Mia Farrow

The only place in the world where a man can get stabbed in the back while climbing a ladder.

William Faulkner

I've been asked if I ever get the DTs. I don't know; it's hard to tell where Hollywood ends and the DTs begin.

W. C. Fields

You can't find true affection in Hollywood because everyone does the fake affection so well.

Carrie Fisher

They've got great respect for the dead in Hollywood, but none for the living.

Errol Flynn

Hollywood is the only place where you can wake up in the morning and hear the birds coughing in the trees.

Joe Frisco

There'll always be an England, even if it's in Hollywood.

Bob Hope

Hollywood is where they write the alibis before they write the story.

Carole Lombard

In Hollywood, brides keep the bouquets and throw away the groom.

Groucho Marx

Over in Hollywood they almost made a great picture, but they caught it in time.

Wilson Mizner

Hollywood's a place where they'll pay you a thousand dollars for a kiss and fifty cents for your soul.

Marilyn Monroe

The only "ism" Hollywood believes in is plagiarism.

Dorothy Parker

Hollywood is an extraordinary kind of temporary place.

John Schlesinger

The only way to be a success here is to be as obnoxious as the next guy.

Sylvester Stallone

Hollywood is loneliness beside the swimming pool.

Liv Ullman

Where they place you under contract instead of observation.

Walter Winchell

A town that has to be seen to be disbelieved.

Walter Winchell

In Hollywood all marriages are happy. It's trying to live together afterwards that causes problems.

Shelley Winters

ACTORS AND ACTING

A celebrity is a person whose name is in everything except the phone directory.

Anonymous

Man dreads fame as a pig dreads fat.

Chinese proverb

A celebrity is a person who works hard all his life to become well-known, and then wears dark glasses to avoid being recognized.

Fred Allen

I can't think of anything grimmer than being an aging actress—God! it's worse than being an aging homosexual.

Candice Bergen

You're not a star until they can spell your name in Karachi.

Humphrey Bogart

An actor is a guy who, if you ain't talking about him, ain't listening.

Marlon Brando

Acting is all about honesty. If you can fake that, you've got it made.

George Burns

On an actor who shot his brains out in a suicide—
He must have been a marvelous shot.

Noël Coward

Modesty is the artifice of actors, similar to passion in call girls.

Jackie Gleason

Actors are only honest hypocrites.

William Hazlitt

Acting is the most minor of gifts and not a very high-class way to earn a living. After all, Shirley Temple could do it at the age of four.

Katharine Hepburn

Life's what's important. Walking, houses, family. Birth and pain and joy. Acting's just waiting for a custard pie. That's all.

Katharine Hepburn

An actor can remember his briefest notice well into senescence and long after he had forgotten his phone number and where he lives.

> *Jean Kerr, 'Please Don't*
> *Eat the Daisies' (1957)*

Acting is like letting your pants down: you're exposed.

> *Paul Newman,*
> *'Time' (1982)*

In the old days an actress tried to become a star. Today we have stars trying to become actresses.

> *Sir Laurence Olivier*

I made the mistake early in my career, when I moved to Hollywood, of being attracted to actresses. I used to go out exclusively with actresses and other female impersonators.

> *Mort Sahl (1976)*

You can pick out actors by the glazed look that comes into their eyes when the conversation wanders away from them.

> *Michael Wilding*

Woody Allen *(b 1935)*
His Kraft is Ebing.

Margot Kernan (1984)

Julie Andrews *(b 1934)*
'The Sound of Music' (1965)—She is like a nun with a switchblade.

Anonymous

'The Tamarind Seed' (1974)—One wishes Miss Andrews didn't always give the impression that she had just left her horse in the hallway.

Michael Billington

'The Sound of Music'—Working with her is like being hit over the head with a Valentine card.

Christopher Plummer

Fred Astaire *(1889-1987)*
I can sing as well as Fred Astaire can act.

Burt Reynolds

Tallulah Bankhead *(1903-68)*
More of an act than an actress.

Anonymous

After a series of poor performances in 'The Exciters'—
Don't look now, Tallulah, but your show's slipping.

                                        Heywood Broun

Miss Bankhead isn't well enough known nationally to
warrant my imitating her.
                                        Bette Davis

John Barrymore   *(1882-1942)*
'My Dear Children'—I always said that I'd like Barrymore's acting till the cows came home. Well, ladies and
gentlemen, last night the cows came home.

                                        George Jean Nathan

Warren Beatty   *(b 1937)*
You're so vain. You probably think this song is about
you.
                                        Carly Simon,
                                        "You're So Vain" (1972)

Robbie Benson   *(b 1956)*
Cute as Bambi and twice as smarmy.

                                        Anonymous

Marlon Brando   *(b 1924)*
Actors like him are good but on the whole I do not
enjoy actors who seek to commune with their armpits,
so to speak.

Greer Garson

Most of the time he sounds like he has a mouth full of
wet toilet paper.

Rex Reed

Charlie Chaplin   *(1889-1977)*
If people don't sit at Chaplin's feet, he goes out and
stands where they are sitting.

Herman J. Mankiewicz

When Chaplin found a voice to say what was on his
mind, he was like a child of eight writing lyrics for
Beethoven's Ninth.

Billy Wilder

John Cleese   *(b 1939)*
He emits an air of overwhelming vanity combined with
some unspecific nastiness, like a black widow spider in
heat. But nobody seems to notice. He could be reciting
'Fox's Book of Martyrs' in Finnish and these people
would be rolling out of their seats.

Roger Gellert,
'The New Statesman'

Joan Collins   *(b 1933)*
She looks like she combs her hair with an eggbeater.

Louella Parsons

Sean Connery   *(b 1929)*
On meeting the leading man in his 007 films—I'm looking for Commander James Bond, not an overgrown stunt man.

Ian Fleming

Gary Cooper   *(1901-61)*
He got a reputation as a great actor just by thinking hard about the next line.

King Vidor

Joan Crawford   *(1906-77)*
The best time I had with Joan Crawford was when I pushed her down the stairs in 'Whatever Happened to Baby Jane?'

Bette Davis

On Crawford's biographies (by Christina Crawford and Bob Thomas)—On closing these two books, a reader senses that Joan Crawford, idol of an age, would have made an exemplary prison matron, possibly at Buchenwald. She had the requisite sadism, paranoia, and taste for violence.

Harriet van Horne,
'New York Post' (1978)

Tony Curtis *(b 1925)*
The only trouble with Tony Curtis is that he's only interested in tight pants and wide billing.

> *Billy Wilder*

Marion Davies *(1897–1961)*
She has two expressions—joy and indigestion.

> *Dorothy Parker*

Bette Davis *(1908–89)*
Publicity for 'Beyond the Forest' (1949)—Nobody's as good as Bette when she's bad.

Her career has been recycled more often than the average tire.
> *Vincent Canby*

Doris Day *(b 1924)*
'Romance on the High Seas'—This was Doris Day's first picture—before she became a virgin.

> *Oscar Levant*

James Dean *(1931–55)*
Another dirty shirttail actor from New York.

> *Hedda Hopper*

He was a hero to the people who saw him only as a little waif, when actually he was a pudding of hatred.

Elia Kazan

Bo Derek   *(b 1957)*
She turned down the role of Helen Keller because she couldn't remember the lines.

Joan Rivers

Marlene Dietrich   *(1901-92)*
Age cannot wither her, nor custom stale her infinite sameness.

David Shipman

Faye Dunaway   *(b 1941)*
'The Wicked Lady' *(1982)*—Even such natural activity as breathing now occasions in her a virtuoso display of overacting. Her eyebrows quiver, her eyes pop, her nostrils dilate, and the skin over her cheekbones tightens. When she actually utters a line, it is as if a battalion of signalers have gone simultaneously berserk and are semaphoring delirious messages.

Frank Walker

Shelley Duvall   *(b 1949)*
The worst and homeliest thing to hit the screens since
Liza Minnelli.
John Simon

Clint Eastwood   *(b 1930)*
On Eastwood's running for mayor of Carmel—What
makes him think a middle-aged actor, who's played
with a chimp, could have a future in politics?

Ronald Reagan

Blake Edwards   *(b 1922)*
'A Fine Mess' (1986)—Clever of Blake Edwards to review his frenetic comedy in the title.

Don Atyeo, 'Time Out'

Dame Edith Evans   *(1888-1976)*
To me, Edith looks like something that would eat its
young.
Dorothy Parker

Mia Farrow   *(b 1945)*
On Farrow's marriage to Frank Sinatra—Hah! I always knew Frank would end up in bed with a boy!

Ava Gardner

Farrah Fawcett *(b 1947)*
Maybe it's the hair. Maybe it's the teeth. Maybe it's the intellect. No, it's the hair.
Tom Shales

Harrison Ford *(b 1942)*
'Hanover Street' (1979)—Costar Harrison Ford, as Lesley-Anne Downs's GI lover, gets our Ryan O'Neal Underacting Award for 1979 . . . and '80 . . . '81.

Rona Barrett

John Ford *(1895–1973)*
John is half-tyrant, half-revolutionary; half-saint, half-satan; half-possible, half-impossible; half-genius, half-Irish.
Frank Capra

Zsa Zsa Gabor *(b 1919)*
She has discovered the secret of perpetual middle age.

Oscar Levant

Greta Garbo *(1905–90)*
Boiled down to essentials, she is a plain mortal with large feet.
Herbert Kretzmer

Judy Garland   *(1922-69)*
I didn't know her well, but after watching her in action I didn't want to know her well.

Joan Crawford

An Angel—with spurs.

Joe Pasternak

Betty Grable   *(1916-73)*
Miss Grable's beauty—if that is the word for it—was of the common sort. Nor did she offer much in the way of character maturity. She was, at best, a sort of great American floozie, and her appeal to lonely GIs was surely that of every hash-house waitress with whom they ever flirted.

Richard Schickel

Farley Granger   *(b 1925)*
'Pride and Prejudice'—He played Mr. Darcy with all the flexibility of a telegraph pole.

Brooks Atkinson (1956)

Cary Grant   *(1904-86)*
You're too bowlegged and your neck is far too thick.

Anonymous Paramount executive at screen test

Rita Hayworth   *(1918–87)*
The audience was reserved and quietly attentive—until Rita Hayworth danced onto the screen in a flaming red dress, cut to show a major part of her acting ability.

Gerald Lieberman

Audrey Hepburn   *(1929–93)*
A walking x-ray.

Oscar Levant

Katharine Hepburn   *(b 1907)*
A cross between Donald Duck and a Stradivarius.

Anonymous

'The Lake'—Go to the Martin Beck Theatre and watch Katharine Hepburn run the gamut of emotion from A to B.

Dorothy Parker,
'Life' (1933)

Charlton Heston   *(b 1924)*
'Ben Hur' (1959)—Charlton Heston throws all his punches in the first ten minutes (three grimaces and two intonations) so that he has nothing left long before he stumbles to the end, four hours later, and has to

react to the crucifixion. (He does make it clear, I must admit, that he disapproves of it.)

Dwight MacDonald (1964)

Van Johnson   *(b 1916)*
Van Johnson does his best: appears.

Caroline A. Lejeune

Diane Keaton   *(b 1946)*
In real life, Keaton believes in God. But she also believes that the radio works because there are tiny people inside it.

Woody Allen (1975)

An acting style that's really a nervous breakdown in slow motion.

John Simon

Alan Ladd   *(1913–64)*
Alan Ladd is hard, bitter, and occasionally charming, but he is, after all, a small boy's idea of a tough guy.

Raymond Chandler

Jessica Lange   *(b 1949)*
'King Kong' (1976)—A dumb blonde who falls for a huge plastic finger.

Judith Crist,
'Saturday Review'

Jack Lemmon　*(b 1925)*
He has a gift for butchering good parts while managing
to look intelligent, thus constituting Hollywood's abid-
ing answer to the theater.
Wilfrid Sheed

Sophia Loren　*(b 1934)*
She is quite impossible to photograph, too tall, too big-
boned, too heavy all around. The face is too short, the
mouth is too wide, the nose is too long.

Screen-test cameraman

Jayne Mansfield　*(1932–67)*
Dramatic art in her opinion is knowing how to fill a
sweater.
Bette Davis

Miss United Dairies herself.
David Niven

Dean Martin　*(b 1917)*
'The Ambushers' (1967)—Martin's acting is so inept
that even his impersonation of a lush seems unconvinc-
ing.
Harry Medved

Mary Martin　*(1913–90)*
She is OK, if you like talent.
Ethel Merman

James Mason   *(1909-84)*
'The Marriage Go Round' (1961)—An actor who couldn't crack a joke if he was a lichee nut.

'Time'

Walter Matthau   *(b 1920)*
He looked like a half-melted rubber bulldog.

John Simon

He is about as likely a candidate for superstardom as the neighborhood delicatessen man.

'Time'

Victor Mature   *(b 1915)*
'Samson and Delilah' (1949)—Mature looks as constipated as ever.

'Time Out'

Steve McQueen   *(1930-80)*
His features resembled a fossilized washrag.

Alan Brien

Ethel Merman   *(1909-84)*
'Gypsy' (1959)—Brassy, brazen witch on a mortgaged broomstick, a steamroller with cleats.

Walter Kerr

Bette Midler   *(b 1944)*
'The Divine Miss M'—Her eyebrows are clipped paren-
theses, and she paints her face for the last days of the
Weimar Republic. Frizzy orange curls grow in her wild
hair like snapdragons pleading for water.

> *Paul Gardner,*
> *'New York Times' (1972)*

Liza Minnelli   *(b 1946)*
She has only two things going for her—a father and a
mother.
> *John Simon*

Marilyn Monroe   *(1926–62)*
A broad with a big future behind her.

> *Constance Bennett*

It's like kissing Hitler.
> *Tony Curtis*

She was good at being inarticulately abstracted for the
same reason that midgets are good at being short.

> *Clive James, 'At the*
> *Pillars of Hercules'*

I don't think she could act her way out of a paper script. She has no charm, delicacy, or taste. She is just an arrogant little tail twitcher who learned to throw sex in your face.

Nunnally Johnson

A vacuum with nipples.

Otto Preminger

Paul Newman   *(b 1925)*
'The Silver Chalice' (1954)—He delivered his lines with the emotional fervor of a conductor announcing local stops.

'The New Yorker'

He has the attention span of a lightning bolt.

Robert Redford (1986)

Margaret O'Brien   *(b 1937)*
If this child had been born in the Middle Ages, she'd have been burned as a witch.

Lionel Barrymore (1943)

Ryan O'Neal   *(b 1941)*
'What's Up, Doc?' (1972)—He is so stiff and clumsy that he can't even manage a part requiring him to be stiff and clumsy.

Jay Cocks

Tatum O'Neal   *(b 1963)*
'Paper Moon' (1973)—All Tatum O'Neal did was to
remind me what a brilliant artist Shirley Temple was.

Lindsay Anderson (1975)

Otto Preminger   *(1906–86)*
He's a horrible man, phew! But who ever hears of him
anymore? Is he dead?
Dyan Cannon

I thank God that neither I nor any member of my
family will ever be so hard up that we have to work for
Otto Preminger.
Lana Turner

Robert Redford   *(b 1936)*
He has turned almost alarmingly blond—he's gone past
platinum, he must be plutonium; his hair is coordi-
nated with his teeth.
Pauline Kael (1976)

Poor little man, they made him out of lemon Jell-O and
there he is. He's honest and he's hard-working. But he's
not great.
Adela Rogers St. John

Diana Rigg   *(b 1938)*
After Rigg appeared nude in 'Abelard and Heloise'—
Diana Rigg is built like a brick mausoleum with insuf-
ficient flying buttresses.

> *John Simon (1970)*

Mickey Rooney   *(b 1920)*
His favorite exercise is climbing tall people.

> *Phyllis Diller*

Dame Margaret Rutherford   *(1892-1972)*
'Murder, She Says' (1962)—A British comedienne
whose appearance suggests an overstuffed electric
chair.

> *'Time'*

Steven Spielberg   *(b 1947)*
Spielberg isn't a filmmaker, he's a confectioner.

> *Alex Cox*

The poet of junk food and pop culture.

> *Sheila Johnston*

Meryl Streep   *(b 1949)*
Oh God! She looks like a chicken.

> *Truman Capote*

She seemed like a frozen, boring blonde, with ice water in her veins; from the Grace Kelly–Tippi Hedren School of Dramatic Art.

Rex Reed

Barbra Streisand   *(b 1942)*
She ought to be called "Barbra Strident."

Stanley Kauffmann

On the set of 'Hello! Dolly,' (1969)—I have more talent in my smallest fart than you have in your entire body.

Walter Matthau

Elizabeth Taylor   *(b 1932)*
She has an insipid double chin, her legs are too short, and she has a slight potbelly.

Richard Burton (1967)

When Elizabeth Taylor meets a man, she takes him and squeezes the life out of him and then throws away the pulp.

Eddie Fisher's mother

Shirley Temple   *(b 1928)*
She wasn't very good. She was fine when she was six or seven. But did you notice how she couldn't act when she was fourteen?

Tatum O'Neal

Jack L. Warner   *(b 1916)*
I can't see what J.W. can do with an Oscar—it can't
say yes.

> *Al Jolson*

Working for Warner Brothers is like f***ing a porcu-
pine. It's a hundred pricks against one.

> *Wilson Mizner*

He never bore a grudge against anyone he wronged.

> *Simone Signoret*

Mae West   *(1892–1980)*
A plumber's idea of Cleopatra.

> *W. C. Fields*

Billy Wilder   *(b 1906)*
At work he is two people—Mr. Hyde and Mr. Hyde.

> *Harry Kurnitz*

Esther Williams   *(b 1923)*
Wet she's a star—dry she ain't.

> *Fanny Brice*

Darryl F. Zanuck   *(1902-79)*
Sam Goldwyn without the accent.

> *Eddie Cantor*

Goodbye, Mr. Zanuck; it certainly has been a pleasure working at Sixteenth Century Fox.

> *Jean Renoir*

COMEDIANS

Steve Allen   *(b 1921)*
When I can't sleep, I read a book by Steve Allen.

> *Oscar Levant*

I'm fond of Steve, but not so much as he is.

> *Jack Paar*

Jack Benny   *(1894-1974)*
When Jack Benny plays the violin it sounds as if the strings are still back in the cat.

> *Fred Allen*

When they asked Jack Benny to do something for the Actors' Orphanage—he shot both his parents and moved in.

Bob Hope

George Burns   *(b 1896)*

George, you're too old to get married again. Not only can't you cut the mustard, honey, you're too old to open the jar.

La Wanda Page

I know George is a great music lover, because a poet once said that every man kills the thing he loves, and I've heard what George does to a song.

Harry Von Zell

Chevy Chase   *(b 1943)*

Chevy Chase couldn't ad-lib a fart after a baked-bean dinner.

Johnny Carson

Phyllis Diller   *(b 1917)*

On Diller's laugh—Like an old Chevrolet starting up on a below-freezing morning.

Anonymous

When she started to play, Steinway came on personally and rubbed his name off the piano.

Bob Hope (1985)

I treasure every moment that I do not see her.

Oscar Levant

Bob Hope   (b 1903)

Bob Hope is still about as funny as he ever was. I just never thought he was that funny in the first place.

Chevy Chase

Oscar Levant   (1906–72)

There's nothing wrong with Oscar Levant that a really first-class miracle couldn't cure.

S. N. Behrman

A character who, if he had not existed, could not be imagined.

S. N. Behrman

Marx Brothers

At the Majestic Theatre, Chicago—The Marx Brothers and several relatives ran around the stage for about an hour—why, I don't know.

Percy Hammond

Chico Marx *(1895-1977)*
Now there sits a man with an open mind. You can feel the draft from here.

Groucho Marx

Groucho Marx *(1890-1977)*
He's a male chauvinistic piglet.

Betty Friedan

Don Rickles *(b 1926)*
He looks like an extra in a crowd scene by Hieronymus Bosch.

Kenneth Tynan,
'The New Yorker' (1978)

Will Rogers *(1879-1935)*
The bosom friend of senators and congressmen was about as daring as an early Shirley Temple movie.

James Thurber

Robin Williams *(b 1951)*
A fellow with the inventiveness of Albert Einstein but the attention span of Daffy Duck.

Tom Shales

6
MUSIC

GENERAL

A musicologist is a man who can read music but can't hear it.

Sir Thomas Beecham

Music hath charm to sooth a savage beast—but I'd try a revolver first.

Josh Billings

Respectable people do not write music or make love as a career.

Alexander Borodin

The Detroit String Quartet played Brahms last night. Brahms lost.

Bennett Cerf

If a literary man puts together two words about music, one of them will be wrong.

Aaron Copland

Composers shouldn't think too much—it interferes with their plagiarism.

Howard Dietz

I hate music, especially when it's played.

Jimmy Durante

Classical music is music written by famous dead foreigners.

Arlene Heath

I occasionally play works by contemporary composers and for two reasons. First to discourage the composer from writing any more and secondly to remind myself how much I appreciate Beethoven.

Jascha Heifitz, 'Life'
(1968)

Song is the licensed medium for bawling in public things too silly or sacred to be uttered in ordinary speech.

Oliver Herford

Classical music is the kind we keep thinking will turn into a tune.

> *Kin Hubbard*

Anybody who has listened to certain kinds of music, or read certain kinds of poetry, or heard certain kinds of performances on the concertina, will admit that even suicide has its brighter aspects.

> *Stephen Leacock*

Every kind of music is good, except the boring kind.

> *Gioacchino Rossini*

Music is essentially useless, as life is.

> *George Santayana*

Too many pieces finish too long after the end.

> *Igor Stravinsky, 'New York Review of Books' (1971)*

If you want to please only the critics, don't play too loud, too soft, too fast, too slow.

> *Arturo Toscanini*

Musical people are so absurdly unreasonable. They always want one to be perfectly dumb at the very moment when one is longing to be absolutely deaf.

> *Oscar Wilde, 'An Ideal*
> *Husband' (1895)*

CLASSICAL COMPOSERS

Johann Sebastian Bach *(1685-1750)*
All Bach's last movements are like the running of a sewing machine.
> *Arnold Bax*

Too much counterpoint; what is worse, Protestant counterpoint.
> *Sir Thomas Beecham*
> *(1971)*

On being asked if Bach was still composing—No madam, he's decomposing.
> *W. S. Gilbert*

Ludwig van Beethoven *(1770-1827)*
Beethoven's last quartets were written by a deaf man and should only be listened to by a deaf man.

> *Sir Thomas Beecham*

'Seventh Symphony'— What can you do with it? It's like a lot of yaks jumping about.

Sir Thomas Beecham

Hector Berlioz   *(1803-69)*

It needs no gift of prophecy to predict that Berlioz will be utterly unknown a hundred years hence to everybody but the encyclopaedists and the antiquarians.

'Boston Daily Advertiser'
(1874)

Berlioz composes by splashing his pen over the manuscript and leaving the issue to chance.

Frédéric Chopin

Berlioz is France's greatest composer, alas. A musician of great genius and little talent.

Maurice Ravel

Pierre Boulez   *(b 1925)*

'Pli Selon Pli'—Pretty monstrous and monstrously pretty.

Igor Stravinsky

Johannes Brahms *(1833–97)*
Proposed sign above a door of Symphony Hall in Boston—Exit in case of Brahms.

Philip Hale

I have played over the music of that scoundrel Brahms. What a giftless bastard! It annoys me that this self-inflated mediocrity is hailed as a genius. Brahms is chaotic and absolutely empty dried-up stuff.

*Peter Ilich Tchaikovsky,
'Diary' (1886)*

Frédéric Chopin *(1810–49)*
'Minute Waltz'—Gives listeners a bad quarter of an hour.

Anonymous

Claude Debussy *(1862–1918)*
Debussy played the piano with the lid down.

Robert Bresson

From "Dawn to Noon on the Sea" from 'La Mer'—I liked the bit about quarter to eleven.

Erik Satie

Fredrick Delius   *(1862–1934)*
The musical equivalent of blancmange.

> *Bernard Levin,*
> *'Enthusiasms' (1983)*

The ugliness of some of his music is really masterly.

> *'The Sun' (1899)*

Charles Gounod   *(1818–93)*
'Redemption'—If you will only take the precaution to
go in long enough after it commences, and to come out
long enough before it is over, you will not find it wear-
isome.

> *George Bernard Shaw*

Edvard Grieg   *(1843–1903)*
'Peer Gynt'—Two or three catch-penny phrases served
up with plenty of orchestral sugar.

> *George Bernard Shaw,*
> *'The World' (1892)*

George Frederick Handel   *(1685–1759)*
A tub of pork and beer.

> *Hector Berlioz*

Handel is only fourth rate. He is not even interesting.

> *Peter Ilich Tchaikovsky*

Gustav Mahler *(1860–1911)*
'*Symphony No. 2*'—If that was music, I no longer understand anything about the subject.

Hans von Bulow

Wolfgang Amadeus Mozart *(1756–91)*
Ah, Mozart! He was happily married—but his wife wasn't.

Victor Borge

Mozart died too late rather than too soon.

Glenn Gould (1984)

It is sobering to consider that when Mozart was my age he had already been dead for a year.

Tom Lehrer

Maurice Ravel *(1875–1937)*
'*Bolero*'—The most insolent monstrosity ever perpetrated in the story of music. From the beginning to the end of its 339 measures it is simply the incredible repetition of the same rhythm and above all it is the blatant recurrence of an overwhelmingly vulgar cabaret tune that is little removed from the wail of an obstreperous back-alley cat.

Edward Robinson, 'The American Mercury' (1932)

Gioacchino Rossini   *(1792-1868)*
Rossini would have been a great composer if his teacher had spanked him enough on the backside.

Ludwig von Beethoven

After Rossini dies, who will there be to promote his music?

Richard Wagner

Arnold Schönberg   *(1874-1951)*
He'd be better off shoveling snow.

Richard Strauss

Franz Schubert   *(1797-1828)*
'Symphony No. 5'—Charming music to hear in a beer garden, with the right company.

Neville Cardus (1938)

Jean Sibelius   *(1865-1957)*
'Symphony No. 6'—I think he must have been drunk when he wrote that.

Benjamin Britten

'Violin Concerto'—A polonaise for polar bears.

Donald F. Tovey

Richard Strauss *(1864-1949)*
If it must be Richard, I prefer Wagner; if it must be Strauss, I prefer Johann.
Anonymous

His absurd cacophony will not be music even in the thirtieth century.
Cesar Cui (1904)

'Elektra'—His Majesty does not know what the [Grenadier Guards] Band has just played, but it is never to be played again.
King George V

'Domestic Symphony'—A cataclysm of domestic plumbing.
H. L. Mencken

Igor Stravinsky *(1882-1971)*
'The Rite of Spring'—Where did these turkeys learn to write music, anyway?
'Comoedia' (1913)

Stravinsky looks like a man who was potty trained too early and that music proves it as far as I am concerned.

Russell Hoban,
'Turtle Diary' (1975)

'*Symphony for Wind—Memory of Debussy*'—I had no idea Stravinsky disliked Debussy as much as this.

> *'Musical Times' (1921)*

His music used to be original. Now it is aboriginal.

> *Sir Ernest Newman,*
> *'Musical Times' (1921)*

Sir Arthur Sullivan   *(1842-1900)*
He is like a man who sits on a stove and then complains that his backside is burning.

> *W. S. Gilbert*

Peter Ilich Tchaikovsky   *(1840-93)*
'*Slavic March*'—One feels that the composer must have made a bet, for all that his professional reputation was worth, that he would write the most hideous thing that had ever been put on paper, and he won it, too.

> *'Boston Evening*
> *Transcript' (1883)*

'*Violin Concerto*'—It gives us, for the first time, the hideous notion that there can be music that stinks to the ear.

> *Eduard Hanslick (1875)*

'First Piano Concerto'—Like the first pancake, it is a
flop.

> N. F. Solviev (1875)

Ralph Vaughan Williams *(1872–1958)*
'Fifth Symphony'—Listening to the 'Fifth Symphony'
of Ralph Vaughan Williams is like staring at a cow for
forty-five minutes.

> *Aaron Copland*

Giuseppe Verdi *(1813–1901)*
When I hear a work I do not like I am convinced it is
my own fault. Verdi is one of those composers.

> *Benjamin Britten*

'Ernani'—It's organ-grinder stuff.

> *Charles Gounod*

Richard Wagner *(1813–83)*
I love Wagner, but the music I prefer is that of a cat
hung up by its tail outside a window and trying to stick
to the panes of glass with its claws.

> *Charles Baudelaire*

If Bach wriggles, Wagner writhes.

> *Samuel Butler,*
> *'Notebooks' (1912)*

Is Wagner a human being at all? Is he not rather a disease? He contaminates everything he touches—he has made music sick. I postulate this viewpoint: Wagner's art is diseased.

Friedrich Nietzsche,
'Der Fall Wagner'

A composer who had some wonderful moments, but awful quarter hours.

Gioacchino Rossini

A composer whose music is better than it sounds.

Mark Twain

I like Wagner's music better than any other music. It is so loud that one can talk the whole time without people hearing what one says.

Oscar Wilde (1891)

OPERA

That was a voice? She sounds like a garbage disposal with a butcher knife caught in it.

Anonymous

Sᴛᴏᴘᴇʀᴀ!

> *Graffiti outside proposed*
> *Dutch opera house*

Nothing is capable of being set to music that is not nonsense.

> *Joseph Addison*

I do not mind what language an opera is sung in so long as it is a language I do not understand.

> *Sir Edward Appleton,*
> *'The Observer' (1955)*

No operatic star has yet died soon enough for me.

> *Sir Thomas Beecham*
> *(1958)*

Opera is a play representing life in another world whose inhabitants have no speech but song, no motions but gestures, and no postures but attitudes. All acting is simulation, and the word simulation is from *simia*, an ape; but in opera the actor takes for his model *Simia audibilis* (or *Pithecanthropus stentor*)—the ape that howls.

> *Ambrose Bierce*

When an opera star sings her head off, she usually improves her appearance.

Victor Borge

Tragic opera is just another disaster aria.

John H. Clark

Swans sing before they die—'twere no bad thing
Should certain persons die before they sing.

Samuel Taylor Coleridge

People are wrong when they say that the opera isn't what it used to be. It is what it used to be. That's what's wrong with it.

Noël Coward

Opera is when a guy gets stabbed in the back and instead of bleeding he sings.

Ed Gardner,
'Duffy's Tavern'

Her singing was mutiny on the high Cs.

Hedda Hopper

In the final analysis, opera is a poor substitute for baseball.

'Los Angeles Herald' (1986)

Opera is people singing when they should be talking.

'*Mail on Sunday*' (1992)

Opera in English is, in the main, just about as sensible as baseball in Italian.

H. L. Mencken

Of all the noises known to man, opera is the most expensive.

Molière

Going to the opera, like getting drunk, is a sin that carries its own punishment with it and that a very severe one.

Hannah More

The opera house is an institution differing from other lunatic asylums in the fact that its inmates have avoided official certification.

Ernest Newman

How wonderful opera would be if there were no singers.

Gioacchino Rossini

Sleep is an excellent way of listening to opera.

James Stephens

In opera, anything that is too stupid to be spoken is sung.

Voltaire

OPERA STARS

Maria Callas   *(1933–77)*
I will not enter into a public feud with Madame Callas, since I am well aware that she has considerably greater competence and experience at that kind of thing than I have.

Rudolf Bing

When Callas carried a grudge, she planted it, nursed it, fostered it, watered it, and watched it grow to sequoia size.

Harold C. Schonberg
(1985)

Enrico Caruso   *(1873–1921)*
'*Madam Butterfly*'—Signor Caruso sang so well that his appearance was easily forgiven but when he was not actually singing, some of the audience were moved to observe that he looked like the Inspector of Police in the first act.

'The (London) Times'
(1905)

Jenny Lind   *(1820–87)*
At the end of the first act we agreed to come away. It
struck me as atrociously stupid. I was thinking of something else the whole time she was jugulating away, and
O! I was so glad to get to the end and have a cigar.

> *William Makepeace*
> *Thackeray (1850)*

Birgit Nilsson   *(b 1918)*
Metropolitan Opera's 'Salome'—Salome was sixteen
and slinky-slim. Birgit Nilsson is forty-six and boats-
wain-burly. As for casting the Swede in the title role of
Richard Strauss's Salome, the idea seemed roughly
comparable to starring Judith Anderson as Lolita.

> *'Time' (1965)*

Luciano Pavarotti   *(b 1935)*
What is or is not art is a matter for personal choice. If
some people want to listen to an overweight Italian
singing in his own language, so be it.

> *Terry Dicks*

Dame Kiri Te Kanawa   *(b 1944)*
A viable alternative to Valium.

> *Ira Siff*

POPULAR MUSIC PERFORMERS

ABC
'Beauty Stab'—It seems that Martin Fry has only succeeded in shooting a poison arrow into his own foot.

> *Errol Somay,*
> *'Rolling Stone'*

AC/DC
'Blow Up Your Video'—Some hints on how to enjoy
this LP. Give your brain the evening off.

> *'Smash Hits'*

Bryan Adams
As far as his love numbers go, I'm afraid someone who
sings like he's got a throat infection is not going to get
me smooching.

> *Laura Lee Davies,*
> *'Time Out'*

The Beach Boys
'Still Cruisin' '—If you've been waiting for the Beach
Boys to hit rock bottom, the suspense is over . . . 'Still
Cruisin' ' is stillborn.

> *Jimmy Guterman,*
> *'Rolling Stone' (1989)*

The Beatles

The Beatles are not merely awful, I would consider it sacrilegious to say anything less than that they are godawful. They are so unbelievably horrible, so appallingly unmusical, so dogmatically insensitive to the magic of the art, that they qualify as crowned heads of antimusic, even as the imposter popes went down in history as antipopes.

William F. Buckley, Jr.,
'On the Right' (1964)

The Bee Gees

'ESP'—Few people know that the CIA is planning to cripple Iran by playing this album on special loudspeakers secretly parachuted into the country.

'Record Mirror' (1988)

Chuck Berry   *(b 1926)*

I think for the life span he's lasted, Chuck Berry's productivity has been nil, more or less.

Elton John

Jon Bon Jovi   *(b 1962)*

'Blaze of Glory'—In comparison, his earlier 'Dead or Alive' sounds like Aaron Copland's 'Appalachian Spring.'

'Entertainment Weekly'
(1990)

Bon Jovi sounds like bad fourth-generation metal, a smudgy Xerox of Quiet Riot.

Jimmy Guterman,
'Rolling Stone'

David Bowie *(b 1947)*
The thin white duke changed musical styles like clothes, seeing rock more as a pose than as internal combustion.

John Milward,
'Rolling Stone'

Chris de Burgh
'Spanish Train and Other Stories'—It sounds almost like the Cat Stevens score to Ingmar Bergman's first rock musical.

Bart Testa, 'Rolling Stone'

Kate Bush
Sort of like the consequences of mating Patti Smith with a Hoover vacuum cleaner.

Dave McGee,
'Rolling Stone'

Cabaret Voltaire
They sound like a Hoover with an old bag screaming over it.

Peter Burns (1987)

The Cars
Anyone with a passable voice and access to a bath could come up with a Cars album in a couple of minutes.

'New Musical Express'

Cheap Trick
'Busted'—If I were a zit-faced, underage dude with a spit-polished Camaro and a cooler full of beers, 'Busted' would make perfect highway fodder to take my mind off the slow clicking of the odometer.

Chuck Dean (1990)

Eric Clapton   *(b 1945)*
If I go 'round to someone's house and there's an Eric Clapton record, I just walk out.

Jon Moss (1985)

The Clash
The sheets of sound they let loose have the cumulative effect of mugging.

'The (London) Times'
(1979)

Leonard Cohen   *(b 1934)*
He gives you the feeling that your dog just died.

'Q' magazine

Perry Como   *(b 1912)*
Perry gave his usual impersonation of a man who has been simultaneously told to say "Cheese" and shot in the back with a poisoned arrow.

Clive James,
'The Observer' (1978)

Elvis Costello   *(b 1955)*
Looks like Buddy Holly after drinking a can of STP Oil Treatment.

Dave Marsh, 'Rolling Stone'

The man who would love to write songs as moving as those that inspired him.

'Sounds'

Roger Daltrey   *(b 1944)*
'Parting Should Be Painless'—Parting with this album should not only be painless but pleasurable.

Parke Puterbaugh,
'Rolling Stone'

John Denver   *(b 1943)*
I'm a John Denver freak, and I don't give a shit that he looks like a f***ing turkey.

Grace Slick

Devo

The five vegetables of the apocalypse.

'New Musical Express'
(1978)

Dr. Feelgood

They sound like sparse backing for a lead singer who never appears.

Charley Walters,
'Rolling Stone'

Duran Duran

A baroque art-rock bubblegum broadcast on a frequency understood only by female teenagers and bred field mice.

Mark Coleman (1987)

Bob Dylan *(b 1941)*

I am unable to see in Dylan anything other than a youth of mediocre talent. Only a completely noncritical audience, nourished on the watery pap of pop music, could have fallen for such tenth-rate drivel.

Ewan MacColl,
'Sing Out' (1965)

Actually, I never liked Dylan's kind of music before; I always thought he sounded just like Yogi Bear.

Mike Ronson

Echo and the Bunnymen
"Ocean Rain"—A monochromatic dirge of banal existential imagery cloaked around the mere skeleton of a musical idea.

> *Parke Puterbaugh,*
> *'Rolling Stone'*

Emerson, Lake and Palmer
'Works'—Appropriately titled, like a tunafish hero sandwich with so much glop on it you forget what you're eating.

> *Bruce Malamut,*
> *'Rolling Stone'*

Energy Orchard
'Stop the Machine'—Nonsense rock for grown-up people with sensible jobs, this is music without anger, edge, excitement, talent, originality, or flair . . . When God invented rock 'n' roll this wasn't really what he had in mind.

> *Ross Fortune,*
> *'Time Out' (1992)*

Eurythmics
'Revenge'—Eurythmics haven't lost their innovative tendencies; they've tied them in neat little packages and made them safe by labeling them. For a group that once managed to subvert new pop formats and still be popular, what kind of revenge is that?

> *Mark Coleman (1986)*

Fabian   *(b 1943)*
This instant asphalt Elvis from Philadelphia.

> *Fred Schruers,*
> *'Rolling Stone'*

Bryan Ferry   *(b 1945)*
He sings like he's throwing up.

> *Andrew O'Connor*

Art Garfunkel   *(b 1941)*
He makes Paul Simon look like LL Cool J.

> *Ian Gittins (1988)*

Generation X
The only punk band with a zero credibility rating . . .
They were no more rebellious than Jason Donovan.

> *Caren Myers (1992)*

Boy George   *(b 1961)*
Boy George is all England needs—another queen who
can't dress.

> *Joan Rivers*

George Harrison   *(b 1943)*
The boy the Beatles called in to make up the numbers.

> *'Melody Maker'*

If you see George Harrison, you can tell him that I think he's a load of old rope.

Cliff Richard

Jimi Hendrix   *(1942-70)*

[He] played guitar like a man possessed but you wished he'd put it back in his pants and have a cup of tea or something . . . The guitar-as-phallus technique never struck me as graceful or beguiling. And, yes, he was dextrous, but so presumably is [magician] Paul Daniels.

Chris Roberts, 'Melody Maker' (1992)

The Jimi Hendrix Experience

A triptych of smirking simian faces . . . The Experience's destruction is inevitable rather than accidental, the surfacing of a violent streak that has always run through rock and roll, the spontaneous violence of the young.

'Newsweek'

Herman's Hermits

"Henry the Eighth"—It would be cheaper, and no more unpleasant, to record yourself in the shower while holding your nose.

Dave Marsh, 'Rolling Stone'

Buddy Holly *(1936–59)*
The biggest no-talent I ever worked with.

Paul Cohen (1956)

Billy Idol *(b 1955)*
The Perry Como of Punk.

Johnny Rotten

Julio Iglesias *(b 1943)*
'1100 Bel Air Place'—Julio goes to Hollywood . . . but to little avail. [Despite] the assistance of two dialect coaches, the quavering tones and husky accent of the suave Latin crooner remain frighteningly reminiscent of an overattentive Spanish waiter who's coming on a bit amorous.

Tom Hibbert (1984)

Michael Jackson *(b 1958)*
'Moonwalker: The Movie' *(1988)*—Altogether a ghastly experience, which even the rabid eleven-year-old in your life might well find patronizing and unimaginative.

Nick Coleman, 'Time Out'

'Remember the Time' *(1992)*—Remember the time when you used to make decent f***ing records?

Alexander O'Neal

He's a great singer—but he's not the most masculine guy, is he?

Alexander O'Neal

The beige chanteur, the Caucasian Diva.

'Punch' (1992)

Whacko Jacko!

'The Sun'

Mick Jagger *(b 1943)*
Mick Jagger—isn't he that motorcycle rider?

Gerald Ford

He sees all women as tarts.

Bianca Jagger

He moves like a parody between a majorette girl and Fred Astaire.

Truman Capote

Grace Jones *(b 1953)*
No-talent singer whose camp posturing made her a Bette Midler–style favorite with the gay community. You had to be there, I guess.

John Swenson,
'Rolling Stone'

Tom Jones   *(b 1940)*
His triumphs in singles like "It's Not Unusual" and "Delilah" have earned him a permanent niche in the annals of nursing-home rock.

John Swenson,
'Rolling Stone'

Janis Joplin   *(1943–70)*
I couldn't stand Janis Joplin's voice . . . She was just a screaming little loudmouthed chick.

Arthur Lee

Kiss
Rock 'n' roll is just mindless fun, the whole f***ing thing is a poetic invention, a grandchild of the whole Dada/Surrealist movement. Rock 'n' roll thrives on negative energy. Those guys in Kiss couldn't wipe their ass by themselves.

Alan Lanier

Kraftwerk
'Autobahn'—Valuable as both a musical oddity and background music for watching tropical fish sleep.

Alan Niester, 'Rolling Stone'

Billy La Bounty
It's only when you hear a pop singer this bad that you can completely appreciate how skillful—I didn't say good—hacks like Barry Manilow and Tony Orlando are.

Dave Marsh, 'Rolling Stone'

John Lennon   *(1940-80)*
'Imagine' (the movie)—It's a lesson in how to use celluloid to create your own personal version of reality. But then, when did Lennon ever truly deal with reality?

Mal Peachey,
'Time Out' (1988)

Liberace   *(1919-87)*
A deadly, winking, sniggering, snuggling, chromium-plated, scent-impregnated, luminous, quivering, giggling, mincing heap of mother love.

William Connor,
'Daily Mirror' (1956)

On bad reviews for his 1954 Madison Square Garden concert—What the critics said hurt me very much. I cried all the way to the bank.

Liberace

Lynyrd Skynyrd

Playing "Free Bird," Lynyrd Skynyrd were utterly horrible. Playing anything else they're merely a competent barroom boogie band.

'New Musical Express'

Paul McCartney   *(b 1942)*

I'd join a band with John Lennon any day, but I wouldn't join a band with Paul McCartney.

George Harrison

Do you think Paul McCartney makes records just to annoy me personally, or does he want to get up everyone's f***ing nose with his f***ing antics?

Alex Harvey

'Give My Regards to Broad Street'—You didn't have to play this movie backward to know that Paul is dead.

'Washington Post' (1985)

Malcolm McLaren

'Round the Outside'—McLaren is a cultural kleptomaniac . . . you should also know that McLaren sings and plays as much on this album as Milli Vanilli did on theirs.

Jim Farber (1991)

Madonna *(b 1958)*

Armed with a wiggle and a Minnie Mouse squawk, she is coarse and charmless.

Sheila Johnston (1987)

She is closer to organized prostitution than anything else.

Morrissey (1986)

She is so hairy—when she lifted up her arm, I thought it was Tina Turner in her armpit.

Joan Rivers

The Monkees

You can't get the Monkees back together as a rock 'n' roll group. That would be like Raymond Burr opening up a law practice.

Michael Nesmith

Morrissey

Morrissey lays out his life like a shoebox full of faded snapshots.

Rolling Stone

Willie Nelson *(b 1933)*

Q: What has 300 legs and 7 teeth?
A: The front row at a Willie Nelson concert.

'Playboy' (1988)

Olivia Newton-John *(b 1947)*
If white bread could sing it would sound like Olivia Newton-John.

Anonymous

Sinéad O'Connor *(b 1966)*
The female Johnny Rotten of the eighties.

'New Musical Express'

Yoko Ono *(b 1933)*
Her voice sounded like an eagle being goosed.

Ralph Novak,
'People' (1985)

If I found her floating in my pool, I'd punish my dog.

Joan Rivers (1983)

Donny Osmond *(b 1957)*
Prima Donny . . . all eyes, sob, and slop. He couldn't open his yap without referring to his tender years; he had teeth like so many well-kept tombstones, and all the soul of one.

Julie Burchill

Marie Osmond *(b 1959)*
She is so pure, Moses couldn't even part her knees.

Joan Rivers

Pink Floyd
'Pink Floyd—The Wall' (movie)—Crossing 'Privilege'
with 'Tommy' couldn't result in anything shallower. All
in all, it's just another flick to appall.

> *Paul Taylor,*
> *'Time Out' (1982)*

The Pogues
'Completely Pogued' (movie)—Even if you have absolutely no interest in the music, the vast array of pasty-
faced uglies is really quite stunning.

> *Laura Lee Davies,*
> *'Time Out' (1989)*

Elvis Presley   *(1935-77)*
I've found someone to replace Tony Curtis as the
world's worst actor—Elvis Presley.

> *Anonymous*

Presley sounded like Jayne Mansfield looked—blowsy
and loud and low.
> *Julie Burchill*

He never contributed a damn thing to music.

> *Bing Crosby*

'Spinout' (movie)—For Presley immobility may signify maturity. He is pitching his act at some sort of adult audience—possibly adult chimpanzees . . . about all he does on the screen is waggle an aggressive guitar and, in an electronically reconstituted baritone, belt out a series of steamy lyrics.

'Time' (1966)

Johnnie Ray
He was the Jayne Mansfield of pop, totally dumb and unautonomous and out of control with no redeeming merit whatsoever—no voice, no songs, no music.

Julie Burchill

Helen Reddy *(b 1942)*
The queen housewife of rock.

Kim Fowley

Lou Reed *(b 1944)*
On finishing the production for the album 'Berlin'—
All right, wrap up this turkey before I puke.

Bob Ezrin

Keith Richards *(b 1943)*
Even the deaf would be traumatized by prolonged exposure to the most hideous croak in Western culture. Richards's voice is simply horrible.

Nick Coleman, 'Time Out'

Lionel Richie   *(b 1949)*
He's got a chin like an ironing board.

Pete Burns (1984)

Kenny Rogers   *(b 1938)*
The musical equivalent of a black-velvet Elvis, the embodiment of schlock art.

Alanna Nash (1990)

The Rolling Stones
The band is now basically a T-shirt selling machine. Jumping Jack Flash no more—more like Limping Hack Flash.

Julie Burchill, 'Mail on Sunday' (1992)

They look like boys whom any self-respecting mum would lock in the bathroom.

'Daily Express' (1964)

The singer will have to go.

Eric Easton (1963)

You walk out of the Amphitheatre after watching the Rolling Stones perform and suddenly the Chicago stockyards smell clean and good by comparison.

Tom Fitzpatrick, 'Chicago Sun-Times'

Linda Ronstadt   *(b 1946)*
'Canciones de mi Padre'—Along comes her album of
Mexican folksongs and ballads, complete with a cover
that make her look like an El Torrito waitress who's
been nibbling the guacamole.

> *David Browne,*
> *'Rolling Stone' (1988)*

Johnny Rotten (Johnny Lydon)
Prince Charmless.

> *Michael Azzerad (1988)*

I can imagine him becoming a successful hair-
dresser—a singing Vidal Sassoon.

> *Malcolm McLaren*

Todd Rundgren   *(b 1948)*
If Rundgren ever has anything approaching a major hit,
it will be totally by accident.

> *'New Musical Express'*

The Sex Pistols
The Sex Pistols do as much for music as World War II
did for peace.

> *'Melody Maker' (1976)*

Grace Slick *(b 1939)*
She is like somebody's mom who'd a few too many drinks at a cocktail party.

Nick Lowe

The Smiths
Drab music for drab people.

Tony James (1985)

Spandau Ballet
'Parade'—Even if Spandau Ballet were to become great at what it does, what it does would still be the most cretinous sort of Anglo-yuppie muzak imaginable.

Kurt Loder, 'Rolling Stone'

Bruce Springsteen *(b 1949)*
He is a glorified gutter rat from a dying New Jersey town who walks with an easy swagger that is part residual stage presence, part boardwalk braggadocio.

Jay Cocks, 'Time' (1975)

After allowing 2 Live Crew to use his song "Born in the USA" for their anti-censorship rap "Banned in the USA"—Dear Mr. Springsteen, I would suggest 'Raped in the USA' as your next album . . . You're now harmful to the women and children who have bought your albums.

Jack Thompson (1990)

Rod Stewart *(1945)*
He was so mean it hurt him to go to the bathroom.

Britt Eklund

Sting *(b 1952)*
Somebody should clip Sting around the head and tell
him to stop singing in that ridiculous Jamaican accent.

Elvis Costello

The Stranglers
Hippies with their hair cut off to make some money.

Boy George (1983)

'*Golden Brown*'—A record to make the Stranglers cult
heroes with Julio Iglesias fans.

Colin Irwin (1982)

Joe Strummer *(b 1953)*
He makes Andy Capp look like a radio announcer.

Dave Marsh, 'Rolling Stone'

Talk Talk
Talk Talk are yet another white synthesizer pop group
complete with a singer (Mark Hollis) who wants to be
Bryan Ferry.

Josephine Hocking

The Talking Heads
'*Naked*'—It's great that the Heads have the freedom to create the sort of record they want, but it's dull to listen to.

> '*Record Mirror*'

Tears for Fears
If honesty were compulsory, every TFF song would be called "Laughing and Singing All the Way to the Bank."

> *David Stubbs,*
> '*Melody Maker*' *(1992)*

The Temptations
At worst, soporific; at best, pleasantly soporific.

> '*New Musical Express*'

Toto
Formula pop singing that wouldn't go over in a Holiday Inn cocktail lounge.

> *Dave Marsh,* '*Rolling Stone*'

Pete Townshend   *(b 1945)*
He is so talentless, and as a lyricist he's so profoundly untalented and philosophically boring to say the least.

> *Lou Reed*

Tina Turner *(b 1939)*
All legs and hair with a mouth that could swallow the whole stadium and the hot-dog stand.

> *Laura Lee Davies,*
> *'Time Out'*

U2
Music for plumbers and bricklayers.

> *Ian McCulloch (1984)*

Victor (formerly Prince) *(b 1959)*
He looks like a dwarf who's been dipped in a bucket of pubic hair.

> *Boy George (1986)*

Bambi with testosterone.

> *Owen Gleiberman,*
> *'Entertainment Weekly'*
> *(1990)*

Roger Waters
Not so much "Another Brick in the Wall," but another prick with a haul!

> *Anonymous*

"The Wall: Berlin" concert—It was going to be a very symbolic, a poignant celebration of the fact that the Berlin Wall was brought down. But it wasn't at all what it was supposed to be. The audience hadn't a clue what was going on . . . Masturbation, that's what it was.

Sinéad O'Connor (1990)

Frank Zappa   *(b 1940)*

Frank Zappa is probably the single most untalented person I've heard in my life. He's two-bit, pretentious, academic, and he can't play his way out of anything. He can't play rock 'n' roll, because he's a loser. And that's why he dresses so funny. He's not happy with himself, and I think he's right.

Lou Reed

Frank Zappa couldn't write a decent song if you gave him a million and a year on an island in Greece.

Lou Reed

ZZ Top

'Fandango'—Rock and roll can be mindless fun, but it never deserved to be this empty-headed.

Dave Marsh, 'Rolling Stone'

7
THE MEDIA

THE PRESS

Doctors bury mistakes. Lawyers hang them. But journalists put theirs on the front page.

Anonymous

The mission of the modern newspaper is to comfort the afflicted and afflict the comfortable.

Anonymous

Tabloids are fast reading for the slow thinking.

Anonymous

I keep reading between the lies.

Goodman Ace

He had been kicked in the head by a mule when young, and believed everything he read in the Sunday papers.

George Ade

In the U.S. today we have more than our share of nattering nabobs of negativism. They've formed their own 4-H club—the hopeless, hysterical, hypochondriacs of history.

Spiro Agnew (1970)

Newspaper strikes are a relief.

Princess Anne

The most important service rendered by the press and the magazines is that of educating people to approach printed matter with distrust.

Samuel Butler

Journalism is the only job that requires no degrees, no diplomas, and no specialized knowledge of any kind.

Patrick Campbell

I love the weight of American Sunday newspapers. Pulling them up off the floor is good for the figure.

Noël Coward

A newspaper is the lowest thing there is!

Richard J. Daley

A newspaper editor is a person who knows precisely what he wants but isn't quite sure.

Walter Davenport

An editor should have a pimp for a brother so he'd have someone to look up to.

Gene Fowler

Editors used to be known by their authors; now some of them are known by their restaurants.

Robert Giroux

The freedom of the press works in such a way that there is not much freedom from it.

Princess Grace of Monaco

The most truthful part of a newspaper is the advertisements.

Thomas Jefferson

The fact that a man is a newspaper reporter is evidence of some flaw of character.

Lyndon B. Johnson

I always said that when we don't have to go through you bastards, we can really get our story over to the American people.

John F. Kennedy (1962)

At a sports press conference—When I say "start" let's have five seconds of silence. [Pause] That's pretty good. That gives something for the news media to quote with absolute accuracy.

Bobby Knight (1982)

The most guileful among the reporters are those who appear friendly and smile and seem to be supportive. They are the ones who will seek to gut you on every occasion.

Ed Koch,
'New York Times' (1984)

Journalists write because they have nothing to say, and have something to say because they write.

Karl Kraus

The press is like the peculiar uncle you keep in the attic—just one of those unfortunate things.

G. Gordon Liddy

People everywhere confuse what they read in newspapers with news.

A. J. Liebling (1956)

Freedom of the press is guaranteed to those who own one.

A. J. Liebling

Newspapermen ask dumb questions. They look up at the sun and ask you if it is shining.

Charles "Sonny" Liston

You should believe all you read in the newspapers, as this makes them more interesting.

Dame Rose Macaulay

The day you write to please everyone you no longer are in journalism. You are in show business.

Frank Miller, Jr.

One of the unsung freedoms that go with a free press is the freedom not to read it.

Ferdinand Mount,
'Daily Telegraph' (1986)

Looking at yourself through the media is like looking at one of those rippled mirrors in an amusement park.

Edmund Muskie,
'Newsweek' (1980)

People in the media say they must look at the president with a microscope. Now I don't mind a microscope, but boy, when they use a proctoscope, that's going too far.

Richard Nixon (1984)

The word media is plural for mediocre.

Rene Saguisag (1987)

The media. It sounds like a convention of spiritualists.

Tom Stoppard,
'Jumpers' (1972)

A foreign correspondent is someone who flies around from hotel to hotel and thinks that the most interesting thing about any story is the fact that he has arrived to cover it.

Tom Stoppard,
'Night and Day' (1978)

Mother [Bess Truman] considered a press conference on a par with a visit to a cage of cobras.

Margaret Truman

Journalism is the ability to meet the challenge of filling space.

Rebecca West

In the old days men had the rack. Now they have the press.

Oscar Wilde (1891)

Most rock journalism is people who can't write interviewing people who can't talk for people who can't read.

Frank Zappa

JOURNALISTS AND PUBLISHERS

Anonymous
On a sycophantic columnist—I see her as one great stampede of lips directed at the nearest derriere.

Noël Coward

Jack Anderson   *(b 1922)*
Jack Anderson is the lowest form of human being to walk the earth. He's a muckraker who lies, steals, and . . . he'll go lower than dog shit for a story.

J. Edgar Hoover

Ambrose Bierce   *(1842–1914)*
He was an all-inclusive cynic.

C. Hartley Grattan

there was no more discretion in Bierce than you will find in a runaway locomotive.

H. L. Mencken

Anthony Burgess   *(b 1917)*
After an 'Observer' interview—He put words into my mouth which I had to look up in the dictionary.

Graham Greene (1982)

William Randolph Hearst   *(1863–1951)*
He wrote so much about the Yellow Peril that his journalism took its distinctive coloration from the subject.

Richard Armour

Hugh Hefner   *(b 1926)*
If Hugh Hefner truly thinks that being spread-eagled is so fantastic, how come we haven't seen his little wahoo with a staple in the middle?

"Designing Women,"
CBS-TV

Dorothy Kilgallen   *(1913–65)*
Dorothy Kilgallen is the only woman I wouldn't mind my wife catching me with. I don't know why she took

such umbrage at my comments on birth control, she's such a living argument for it.

Johnny Carson

Walter Lippmann *(1889–1974)*

Lippmann was a true muckraker, a muckraker on the global scale, a man who knew that when statesmen prepare to commit genocide they come to the green baize table in striped pants and morning coats.

Harrison E. Salisbury
(1974)

Henry Luce *(1898–1967)*

Mr. Luce's unique contribution to American journalism is that he placed into the hands of the people yesterday's newspaper and today's garbage homogenized into one neat package.

Herblock

Robert McCormick *(1849–1919)*

The great, overgrown lummox of a Colonel Robert McCormick, mediocre in ability, less than average in brains, and a damn physical coward in spite of his size, sitting on the tower of the [Chicago] Tribune Building with his guards protecting him while he squirts sewage at men whom he happens to dislike.

Harold L. Ickes (1938)

Joseph Pulitzer   *(1847-1911)*
Undoubtedly semineurasthenic, a disease-demonized
soul, who could scarcely control himself in anything, a
man who was fighting an almost insane battle with life
itself, trying to be omnipotent and what not else, and
never to die.

Theodore Dreiser

Dorothy Thompson   *(1894-1961)*
She is the only woman who had her menopause in
public and got paid for it.

Alice Roosevelt Longworth

TELEVISION

Eyestrain radio.

Anonymous

A box that has changed children from an irresistible
force into an immovable object.

Anonymous

The electronic device that intersperses gory slaughter
with the brushing of teeth.

Anonymous

MTV—a vidiot's delight.

Anonymous

A spirit of national masochism prevails, encouraged by an effete corps of impudent snobs who characterize themselves as intellectuals.

Spiro Agnew (1966)

Television is a device that permits people who haven't got anything to do to watch people who can't do anything. It is radio fluoroscoped; the triumph of machinery over people; a medium because anything good on it is rare.

Fred Allen

In California, they don't throw their garbage away— they make it into TV shows.

Woody Allen

All the music I have ever seen on television looks grotesque. You see right down the larynx, almost into the tummy; the eyes go this way, the nose goes that way, and the mouth is twisted round. The whole thing is revolting. That's television, so far as music is concerned.

Sir Thomas Beecham

Television has a real problem. They have no page two.

Art Buchwald (1959)

Television is democracy at its ugliest.

Paddy Chayefsky

Good heavens, television is something you appear on;
you don't watch it.

Noël Coward

Television is a medium of entertainment which permits
millions of people to listen to the same joke at the
same time and yet remain lonesome.

T. S. Eliot,
'New York Post' (1963)

In America television can make so much money doing
its worst, it cannot afford to do its best.

Fred Friendly (1967)

The news is the one thing the networks can point to
with pride. Everything else they do is crap—and they
know it.

Fred Friendly (1980)

TV is an invention that permits you to be entertained
in your living room by people you wouldn't have in
your home.

David Frost (1971)

I have found the most divine sleeping pill—television.

Eva Gabor

A medium that has raised writing to a new low.

Samuel Goldwyn

Why should people go out and pay to see bad films when they can stay at home and see bad television for nothing?

Samuel Goldwyn

There is something supremely reassuring about television; the worst is always yet to come.

Jack Gould

In the age of television, image becomes more important than substance.

S. I. Hayakawa

Television has done much for psychiatry, by spreading information about it as well as contributing to the need for it.

Alfred Hitchcock

TV is a medium, because it is neither rare nor well done.

Ernie Kovacs

TV has proved that people will look at anything rather than at each other.

Ann Landers

I find television very educating. Every time someone turns on the set I go into the other room and read a book.

Groucho Marx

I have never seen a bad television program, because I refuse to. God gave me a mind, and a wrist to turn things off.

Jack Paar, 'TV Guide'

Television is the bland leading the bland.

Murray Schumach

Dealing with network executives is like being nibbled to death by ducks.

Eric Sevareid

If you read a lot of books, you're considered well read. But if you watch a lot of TV, you're not considered well viewed.

Lily Tomlin

Acting on television is like being asked by the captain to entertain the passengers while the ship goes down.

Peter Ustinov (1957)

Perhaps the crime situation would be improved if we could get more cops off television and onto the streets.

Bill Vaughan,
'Kansas City Star'

Television is a twenty-one-inch person. I'm delighted with it, because it used to be that films were the lowest form of art. Now we've got something to look down on.

Billy Wilder

Television is the plug-in drug.

Marie Winn

Television is chewing gum for the eyes.

Frank Lloyd Wright

I can't understand why anybody would want to devote their life to a cause like dope. It's the most boring pastime I can think of. It ranks a close second to television.

Frank Zappa

TELEVISION PERSONALITIES

We call them Twinkies. You've seen them on television acting the news, modeling and fracturing the news while you wonder whether they've read the news—or if they've blow-dried their brains, too.

Linda Ellerbee,
'And So It Goes' (1986)

Johnny Carson   *(b 1925)*
It has always been my personal conviction that Carson is the most overrated amateur since Evelyn and her Magic Violin.

Rex Reed

He's an anesthetist—Prince Valium.

Mort Sahl

Connie Chung   *(b 1946)*
Is Connie Chung a real journalist or just a reenactment of one?

'Rolling Stone' (1990)

Walter Cronkite   *(b 1916)*
You can learn more by watching "Let's Make a Deal" than you can by watching Walter Cronkite for a month.

Monty Hall

Sam Donaldson   *(b 1934)*
He is television's sultan of splutter.

Hugh Sidey (1985)

David Frost   *(b 1939)*
I always felt Frost was totally absorbed with himself and
had a synthetic personality with a fixed smile carefully
adapted to the slick phoniness of ad-agency types,
show-business types, and broadcast-executive types.

Howard Cosell

Dan Rather   *(b 1931)*
Reporting for "60 Minutes" from Afghanistan—Rather
wore peasant togs that made him look like an extra out
of Doctor Zhivago. Vanessa Redgrave wearing the same
outfit would have been welcomed at any chic party in
Europe. Somehow one got the feeling that this was not
so much Dan Rather as Stuart Whitman playing Dan
Rather. Or Dan Rather playing Stuart Whitman playing
Dan Rather.

Tom Shales,
'Washington Post' (1980)

Geraldo Rivera   *(b 1943)*
If Geraldo Rivera is the first journalist in space, NASA
can test weightlessness on weightlessness.

Anonymous

Andy Rooney   *(b 1920)*

We've all had the experience of listening to him talk until an idea comes along. I don't know how Andy can make 60 seconds on "60 Minutes" seem like 60 hours.

Walter Cronkite

He's a twit. He wastes good airwaves and electrons. He's just plain unbearable.

Jeff Jarvis, 'Entertainment Weekly' (1990)

Dinah Shore   *(b 1917)*

I never watch the Dinah Shore show—I'm a diabetic.

Oscar Levant

Ed Sullivan   *(1901–74)*

Ed Sullivan will be around as long as someone else has talent.

Fred Allen

Barbara Walters   *(b 1931)*

Who would want to bother to try to get along without Barbara Walters? Barbara Walters—manicurist, pedicurist, guru of kitsch, yenta, maven, gadfly, blabbermouth, and Mother Confessor to the world.

*Tom Shales,
'Washington Post' (1980)*

8
EDUCATION

A professor is a man whose job is to tell students how to solve the problems of life which he himself has tried to avoid by becoming a professor.

Anonymous

Parents never appreciate a teacher unless it rains all weekend.

Anonymous

A college dean is a man who doesn't know enough to be a professor but who is too smart to be a president.

Anonymous

More often than not the only thing a man gets out of college is himself.

Anonymous

You can tell a Harvard man, but you can't tell him much.

Anonymous

One of the first things schoolchildren in Texas learn is how to compose a simple declarative sentence without the word "shit" in it.

Anonymous

Nothing in education is so astonishing as the amount of ignorance it accumulates in the form of inner facts.

Henry Adams

I didn't need no diploma to do what I do.

Louis Armstrong

Education is learning what you didn't even know you didn't know.

Daniel F. Boorstin

Most educators would continue to lecture on navigation while the ship is going down.

James H. Boren

The average Ph.D. thesis is nothing but a transference of bones from one graveyard to another.

J. Frank Dobie

A lot of fellows nowadays have a B.A., M.A., or Ph.D. Unfortunately, they don't have a J.O.B.

Fats Domino (1966)

It doesn't make much difference what you study, as long as you don't like it.

Finley Peter Dunne

How long did it take six men to build a wall if three of them took a week? I recall that we spent almost as much time on this problem as the men spent on the wall.

Gerald Durrell

Colleges are like old-age homes, except for the fact that more people die in colleges.

Bob Dylan

Education is the ability to listen to almost anything without losing your temper or your self-confidence.

Robert Frost

Today's children seem to be born with two strikes against them: teachers and school-bus drivers.

Robert Fuoss

A lecture is an occasion when you numb one end to benefit the other.

John Gould

The advantage of a classical education is that it enables you to despise the wealth which it prevents you from achieving.

Russell Green

A diploma is a remembrance of things passed.

Honey Greer

A college is a place where pebbles are polished and diamonds dimmed.

Robert G. Ingersoll

Education is the inculcation of the incomprehensible into the indifferent by the incompetent.

John Maynard Keynes

Stand firm in your refusal to remain conscious during algebra. In real life, I assure you, there is no such thing as algebra.

Fran Lebowitz (1981)

Whenever the cause of the people is entrusted to professors it is lost.

Nikolai Lenin

Teachers are overworked and underpaid. True, it is an exacting and exhausting business, this damming up the flood of human potentialities.

George B. Leonard

Our American professors like their literature clear and cold and pure and dead.

Sinclair Lewis (1930)

He may be dead; or, he may be teaching English.

Cormac McCarthy

Show me a college dean whose professors are out on strike and I'll show you someone who's no longer in possession of his faculties.

Bert Murray

In large states public education will always be medio-cre, for the same reason that in large kitchens the cooking is bad.

Friedrich Nietzsche

A little learning is a dangerous thing.

Alexander Pope

The schools ain't what they used to be and never was.

Will Rogers

Education is one of the chief obstacles to intelligence and freedom of thought.

Bertrand Russell

You don't have to think too hard when you talk to a teacher.

J. D. Salinger

A child only educated at school is an uneducated one.

George Bernard Shaw

He who can, does. He who cannot, teaches.

George Bernard Shaw

Education has produced a vast population able to read but unable to distinguish what is worth reading.

G. M. Trevelyan (1944)

Education is what you must acquire without any interference from your schooling.

Mark Twain

School is where you go between when your parents can't take you and industry can't take you.

John Updike

Teaching has ruined more American novelists than drink.

Gore Vidal, 'Oui' (1975)

It is a pity so many people get college training without getting an education.

'Washington Post'

Education appears to be the thing that enables a man to get along without using his intelligence.

A. E. Wiggan

9
RELIGION

Don't stay away from church because there are so many hypocrites. There's always room for one more.

A. R. Adams

Not only is there no God, but try getting a plumber on weekends.

Woody Allen

On dropping $50 into a Salvation Army tambourine—Don't bother to thank me. I know what a perfectly ghastly season it's been for you Spanish dancers.

Tallulah Bankhead

To pray is to ask that the laws of the universe be annulled on behalf of a single practitioner confessedly unworthy.

Ambrose Bierce

A Christian is one who believes the New Testament is a divinely inspired book admirably suited to the spiritual needs of his neighbor.

Ambrose Bierce

A convent is a place of retirement for women who wish for leisure to meditate upon the vice of idleness.

Ambrose Bierce

A heathen is a benighted creature who has the folly to worship something he can see and can feel.

Ambrose Bierce

A Christian is one who follows the teachings of Christ in so far as they are not inconsistent with a life of sin.

Ambrose Bierce

Religion is excellent stuff for keeping common people quiet.

Napoleon Bonaparte

Christian ethics are seldom found save in the philosophy of some unbeliever.

Heywood Broun

Catholicism is like Howard Johnson [motels], and what they have are these franchises and they give all these people different franchises in different countries but they have one government, and when you buy the Howard Johnson franchise you can apply it to the geography—whatever's cool for the area—and then you, you know, pay the bread to the main office.

Lenny Bruce

Every day people are straying away from the church and going back to God.

Lenny Bruce

An atheist is a man with no visible means of support.

John Buchan

Thank God, I am still an atheist.

Luis Buñuel (1969)

The Bible may be the truth, but it is not the whole truth and nothing but the truth.

Samuel Butler

The problem with born-again Christians is that they are an even bigger pain the second time around.

Herb Caen (1981)

If Jesus were to come today, people would not even crucify him. They would ask him to dinner, and hear what he had to say, and make fun of him.

Thomas Carlyle

It is usually when men are at their most religious that they behave with the least sense and the greatest cruelty.

Ilka Chase

A Puritan is a person who pours righteous indignation into the wrong things.

G. K. Chesterton

Unitarianism is, in effect, the worst kind of atheism joined to the worst of one kind of Calvinism, like two asses tied tail to tail.

Samuel Taylor Coleridge
(1832)

Men will wrangle for religion, write for it, fight for it, die for it, anything but live for it.

Charles Caleb Cotton

I don't believe in God because I don't believe in Mother Goose.

Clarence Darrow

And of all the plagues with which mankind are cursed, Ecclesiastic tyranny's the worst.

Daniel Defoe

The idea of a Supreme Being who creates a world in which one creature is designed to eat another in order to subsist, and then pass a law saying, "Thou shalt not kill," is so monstrously, immeasurably, bottomlessly absurd that I am at a loss to understand how mankind has entertained or given it house room all this long.

Peter De Vries

A dead atheist is someone who's all dressed up with no place to go.

James Duffecy,
'New York Times' (1964)

So far as religion of the day is concerned, it is a damned fake . . . Religion is bunk.

Thomas Edison

Science without religion is lame, religion with science is blind.

Albert Einstein

If men are so wicked with religion, what would they be without it?

Benjamin Franklin

When a man is freed of religion, he has a better chance to live a normal and wholesome life.

Sigmund Freud

Organized Christianity has probably done more to retard the ideals that were its founders' than any other agency in the world.

Richard Le Gallienne

Priests are no more necessary to religion than politicians to patriotism.

John H. Holmes (1933)

A mystic is a person who is puzzled before the obvious but who understands the nonexistent.

Elbert Hubbard

Perhaps the most lasting pleasure in life is the pleasure of not going to church.

William Inge

No man with any sense of humor ever founded a religion.

Robert G. Ingersoll (1884)

In all ages, hypocrites, called priests, have put crowns upon the heads of thieves, called kings.

Robert G. Ingersoll

With soap, baptism is a good thing.

Robert G. Ingersoll

The Bible is nothing but a succession of civil rights struggles by the Jewish people against their oppressors.

Jesse Jackson

'Twas only fear first in the world made gods.

Ben Jonson, 'Sejanus'

I do not believe in God. I believe in cashmere.

Fran Lebowitz

Christianity will go. It will go. It will vanish and shrink. We are more popular than Jesus now. I don't know which will go first—rock and roll or Christianity. Jesus was all right, but his disciples were thick and ordinary.

John Lennon

I do believe our army chaplains, taken as a class, are the worst men we have in our service.

Abraham Lincoln

The New English Bible—Even the end of the world is described as if it were only an exceptionally hot afternoon.

Peter Mallen (1985)

An archbishop is a Christian ecclesiastic of a rank superior to that attained by Christ.

H. L. Mencken

Say what you will about the Ten Commandments, you will always come back to the pleasant fact that there are only ten of them.

H. L. Mencken

Religion is a conceited effort to deny the most obvious realities.

H. L. Mencken

The Creator is a comedian whose audience is afraid to laugh.

H. L. Mencken

The Old Testament is responsible for more atheism, agnosticism, disbelief—call it what you will—than any book ever written; it has emptied more churches than all the counterattractions of cinema, motor bicycle, and golf course.

A. A. Milne

Mormons invented themselves just as other religious and ethnic groups invented themselves. But Mormons did so in such a singularly impressive way that we will probably always remain baffled as to how exactly it happened.

Laurence Moore,
'New York Times' (1985)

Religion is induced insanity.

Madalyn Murray O'Hair

Atheists have an excellent longevity record because we have no place to go after we die, so we take good care of ourselves and our world while we are here.

Madalyn Murray O'Hair

The history of saints is mainly the history of insane people.

Benito Mussolini (1904)

After coming in contact with a religious man I always feel that I must wash my hands.

> *Friedrich Nietzsche,*
> *'The Antichrist' (1888)*

As with the Christian religion, the worst advertisement for Socialism is its adherents.

> *George Orwell (1937)*

Saints should be judged guilty until they are proved innocent.

> *George Orwell (1950)*

The greatest service that could be rendered the Christian peoples would be to convert them to Christianity.

> *'Palatka News'*

Jesus was a crackpot.

> *Bhagwan Shree Rajneesh*

Unlike Christianity, which preached a peace that it never achieved, Islam unashamedly came with a sword.

> *Steven Runciman*

Everyone prefers belief to the exercise of judgment.

> *Seneca*

Christianity might be a good thing if anyone ever tried it.

George Bernard Shaw

The Jews generally give value. They make you pay; but they deliver the goods. In my experience the men who want something for nothing are invariably Christians.

George Bernard Shaw,
'Saint Joan' (1923)

I'm an atheist and I thank God for it.

George Bernard Shaw

If I had been the Virgin Mary, I'd have said, "No!"

Stevie Smith

There are three sexes—men, women, and clergymen.

Sydney Smith

The world is proof that God is a committee.

Bob Stokes

I think there is an immense shortage of Christian charity among so-called Christians.

Harry S. Truman

Man is the only animal that has the true religion—several of them.

Mark Twain

Religion is the source of all imaginable follies and disturbances; it is the parent of fanaticism and civil discord; it is the enemy of mankind.

Voltaire

Christianity must be divine, since it has lasted 1,700 years despite the fact that it is so full of villainy and nonsense.

Voltaire

The Catholic faith is confession on Saturday. Absolution on Sunday. At it again on Monday.

H. G. Wells

The total absence of humor from the Bible is one of the most singular things in literature.

Alfred North Whitehead

I read the Book of Job last night—I don't think God comes well out of it.

Virginia Woolf

10
SCIENCE

GENERAL

Science is the orderly arrangement of what, at the moment, seem to be the facts.

Anonymous

Research is the process of going up alleys to see if they are blind.

Marston Bates

It is inexcusable for scientists to torture animals; let them make their experiments on journalists and politicians.

Henrik Ibsen

In studying the science of yesteryear one comes upon such interesting notions as gravity, electricity, and the roundness of the earth—while an examination of more recent phenomena shows a strong trend towards spray cheese, stretch denim, and the Moog synthesizer.

Fran Lebowitz,
'Metropolitan Life'

I almost think it is the ultimate destiny of science to exterminate the human race.

Thomas L. Peacock (1860)

MEDICINE

Drill, fill, and bill.

Old dental saying

A physician is a man who pours drugs of which he knows little into a body of which he knows less.

Anonymous

A virus is a Latin word translated by doctors to mean "Your guess is as good as mine."

Anonymous

No physician is really good before he has killed one or two patients.

Hindu proverb

If you have a friend who is a physician, send him to the house of your enemy.

Portuguese proverb

Heaven defend me from a busy doctor.

Welsh proverb

We may lay down a maxim, that when a nation abounds in physicians it grows thin of people.

Joseph Addison (1711)

Doctors are the same as lawyers; the only difference is that lawyers merely rob you, whereas doctors rob you and kill you too.

Anton Chekhov,
'Ivanov' (1887)

The best doctor is the one you run for and can't find.

Dennis Diderot

I wonder why you can always read a doctor's bill and you can never read his prescription.

Finley Peter Dunne

Some doctors make the same mistakes for twenty years and call it clinical experience.

Dr. Noah Fabricant

God heals, the doctor takes the fee.

Benjamin Franklin

A doctor is someone who kills you today to prevent you from dying tomorrow.

'Punch'

A male gynecologist is like an auto mechanic who has never owned a car.

Carrie Snow

The art of medicine consists of amusing the patient while nature cures the disease.

Voltaire

PSYCHOLOGY

The science that tells you what you already know in words you don't understand.

Anonymous

Of course behaviorism works. So does torture.

W. H. Auden

Psychology is as unnecessary as directions for using poison.

Karl Kraus

SOCIOLOGY

Sociologists are those academic accountants who think that truth can be shaken from an abacus.

Peter S. Prescott (1972)

The study of people who do not need to be studied by people who do.

E. S. Turner

TECHNOLOGY

One cannot walk through a mass-production factory and not feel that one is in Hell.

W. H. Auden (1953)

Modern technology
Owes ecology
An apology.

Alan M. Eddison,
'Worse Verse' (1969)

Technological progress is like an ax in the hands of a pathological criminal.

Albert Einstein

The marvels of modern technology include the development of a soda can which, when discarded, will last forever—and a $7,000 car which, when properly cared for, will rust out in two or three years.

Paul Harwitz

Technological society has succeeded in multiplying the opportunities for pleasure, but it has great difficulty in generating joy.

Pope Paul VI (1975)

Nothing you can't spell will ever work.

Will Rogers (1924)

Technology is a queer thing. It brings you great gifts with one hand, and it stabs you in the back with the other.

C. P. Snow

11
POLITICS

THANK GOD ONLY ONE OF THEM CAN WIN!

Bumper sticker during
Kennedy-Nixon (1960)
presidential campaign

The first requirement of a statesman is that he be dull. This is not always easy to achieve.

Dean Acheson (1970)

During an election campaign the air is full of speeches and vice versa.

Henry Adams

If I were to go over my life again, I would be a shoe-maker rather than an American statesman.

John Adams

Politics is the gentle art of getting votes from the poor and campaign funds from the rich by promising to protect each from the other.

Oscar Ameringer

Politics, it seems to me, for years, or all too long,
Has been concerned with right or left instead of right
   or wrong.

Richard Armour

Communism—the illegitimate child of Karl Marx and Catherine the Great.

Clement Attlee

Just say the word "politician" and I think of chicanery.

Lucille Ball

The politician is an acrobat. He keeps his balance by saying the opposite of what he does.

Maurice Barres

Politics is a blood sport.

Aneurin Bevan

Politics is the conduct of public affairs for private advantage.

Ambrose Bierce

Einstein's theory of relativity, as practiced by congressmen, simply means getting members of your family on the payroll.

James H. Boren

If God had been a Liberal, we wouldn't have had the Ten Commandments—we'd have the Ten Suggestions.

Malcolm Bradbury

The office of president is such a bastardized thing, half royalty and half democracy, that nobody knows whether to genuflect or spit.

Jimmy Breslin

Anyone that wants the presidency so much that he'll spend two years organizing and campaigning for it is not to be trusted with the office.

David Broder

I always wanted to get into politics, but I was never light enough to make the team.

Art Buchwald

What the liberal really wants is to bring about change which will not in any way endanger his position.

Stokely Carmichael

Democracy means government by the uneducated, while aristocracy means government by the badly educated.

G. K. Chesterton

All that Communism needs to make it successful is somebody to feed and clothe it.

'Columbia Record'

Democracy consists of choosing your dictators, after they've told you what it is you want to hear.

Alan Coren (1975)

The U.S. brags about its political system, but the president says one thing during the election, something else when he takes office, something else during midterm, and something else when he leaves.

Deng Xiaoping

Socialism is Bolshevism with a shave.

'Detroit Journal'

No man should be in public office who can't make more money in private life.

Thomas E. Dewey

In politics there is no honor.

Benjamin Disraeli

Politics makes strange bedfellows.

Charles Dudly

Politics is developing more comedians than radio ever did.

Jimmy Durante

Oh, that lovely title, ex-president.

Dwight D. Eisenhower (1959)

A mugwump is one of those boys who always has his mug on one side of the political fence and his wump on the other.

Albert J. Engel (1936)

The cardinal rule of politics—never get caught in bed with a live man or a dead woman.

J. R. Ewing, "Dallas"

Two cheers for democracy; one because it admits variety and two because it permits criticism. Two cheers are quite enough; there is no occasion to give three.

E. M. Forster (1951)

When a politician changes his position it's sometimes hard to tell whether he has seen the light or felt the heat.

Robert Fuoss

Politics is not the art of the possible. It consists in choosing between the disastrous and the unpalatable.

John Kenneth Galbraith

Nothing is so admirable in politics as a short memory.

John Kenneth Galbraith

I have come to the conclusion that politics are too serious a matter to be left to the politicians.

Charles de Gaulle

Since a politician never believes what he says, he is surprised when others believe him.

Charles de Gaulle

Politics means the art of compromise. Most politicians are all-too-well schooled in this art. They compromise to get nominated; they compromise to get elected; and they compromise time and time again, after they are elected, to stay in office.

Dick Gregory, 'Why I Want to Be President'

A Conservative is a man who is too cowardly to fight and too fat to run.

Elbert Hubbard

Some fellows get credit for being conservative when they are only stupid.

Kin Hubbard

Being president is like being a jackass in a hailstorm. There's nothing to do but stand there and take it.

Lyndon B. Johnson

Mothers all want their sons to grow up to be president but they don't want them to become politicians in the process.

John F. Kennedy

One-fifth of the people are against everything all the time.

Robert Kennedy

I was ashamed of being a Republican and afraid of being a Democrat.

Robert W. Kenny

Politicians are the same all over. They promise to build a bridge even when there's no river.

Nikita Krushchev (1960)

The more I see of the representatives of the people, the more I admire my dogs.

Alphonse de Lamartine

Fascism is Capitalism in decay.

Nikolai Lenin

Elections are held to delude the populace into believing that they are participating in government.

Gerald Lieberman

The candidate never wore diapers as a baby way back
   when;
It seems that no one could ever pin him down, even
   then.
                                   George O. Ludcke

The function of socialism is to raise suffering to a
higher level.
                                   Norman Mailer

Congress is so strange. A man gets up to speak and
says nothing. Nobody listens—and then everybody dis-
agrees.
                                   Boris Marshalov

Being in politics is like being a football coach. You have
to be smart enough to understand the game and stupid
enough to think it's important.

                                   Eugene McCarthy

Democracy is the theory that the common people
know what they want and deserve to get it good and
hard.
                                   H. L. Mencken

A politician is an animal that can sit on the fence and
keep both ears to the ground.

                                   H. L. Mencken

Communism, like any other revealed religion, is largely made up of prophecies.

H. L. Mencken

Bad officials are elected by good citizens who do not vote.

George Jean Nathan

It is no wonder politicians get hard-boiled. They're always in hot water.

'New Orleans Times'

Democracy is finding proximate solutions to insoluble problems.

Reinhold Niebuhr

Lobbyists are people who go to Washington to mix business with pressure.

Lane Olinghouse

Socialism is workable only in heaven, where it isn't needed, and in hell, where they've got it.

Cecil Palmer

Public office is the last refuge of the incompetent.

Boies Penrose

Those who are too smart to engage in politics are punished by being governed by those who are dumber.

Plato

The leaders of the Democratic Party have gone so far left, they've left the country.
Ronald Reagan

A statesman is a successful politician who is dead.

Thomas B. Reed

A conservative is a liberal who got mugged the night before.
Frank Rizzo (1972)

Fascism is above all the unconscious awakening of our profound racial instinct.
Alfredo Rocco

With Congress, every time they make a joke, it's a law, and every time they make a law, it's a joke.

Will Rogers

A conservative is a man with two perfectly good legs who, however, has never learned to walk forward.

Franklin D. Roosevelt

The most successful politician is he who says what everybody else is thinking most often and in the loudest voice.

Theodore Roosevelt

A conservative is someone who believes in reform. But not now.

Mort Sahl

A politician should have three hats. One for throwing in the ring, one for talking through, and one for pulling rabbits out of if elected.

Carl Sandburg

Fascism is Capitalism plus Murder.

Upton Sinclair

Communism is the corruption of a dream of justice.

Adlai Stevenson

Politics is perhaps the only profession for which no preparation is thought necessary.

Robert Louis Stevenson

Government is an association of men who do violence to the rest of us.

Leo Tolstoy

Ninety-eight percent of the adults in this country are decent, hard-working, honest Americans. It's the other lousy two percent that get all the publicity. But then— we elected them.

Lily Tomlin

My choice early in life was either to be a piano player in a whorehouse or a politician. And to tell the truth, there's hardly any difference.

Harry S. Truman

All the president is, is a glorified public relations man who spends his time flattering, kissing, and kicking people to get them to do what they are supposed to do anyway.

Harry S. Truman

The White House is the finest jail in the world.

Harry S. Truman (1949)

Suppose you were an idiot, and suppose you were a member of Congress, but I repeat myself.

Mark Twain

On a recently deceased politician—I did not attend his funeral; but I wrote a nice letter saying I approved of it.

Mark Twain

Two members of the acting profession who are not needed by that profession, Mr. Ronald Reagan and Mr. George Murphy, entered politics, and they've done extremely well. Since there has been no reciprocal tendency in the other direction, it suggests to me that an actor's job is still more difficult than their new one.

Peter Ustinov

Politics is the art of preventing people from busying themselves with what is their own business.

Paul Valéry

Any man who is not something of a socialist before he is forty has no heart. Any man who is still a socialist after he is forty has no head.

Wendell L. Willkie

A conservative is a man who thinks and sits, mostly sits.

Woodrow Wilson

U.S. POLITICIANS

Anonymous
He has every attribute of a dog except loyalty.

Thomas P. Gore

John Adams *(1735-1826)*
He is distrustful, obstinate, excessively vain, and takes no counsel from anyone.

Thomas Jefferson

William Jennings Bryan *(1860-1925)*
One could drive a prairie schooner through any part of his argument and never scrape against a fact.

David Houston

The national tear duct.

H. L. Mencken

Aaron Burr *(1756-1836)*
I never thought him an honest, frank-dealing man, but considered him as a crooked gun or other perverted machine, whose aim or shot you could never be sure of.

Thomas Jefferson (1807)

George Bush   *(b 1924)*
All hat and no cattle.

John Connally

On his tennis style—Real men don't lob.

'Runner's World' (1988)

Jimmy Carter   *(b 1924)*
He would cut the cards if he was playing poker with his mother.

Anonymous

Sometimes when I look at all my children, I say to myself, "Lillian, you should have stayed a virgin."

Lillian Carter

Jimmy Carter as president is like Truman Capote marrying Dolly Parton. The job is too big for him.

Rich Little

If you're in the peanut business, you learn to think small.

Eugene McCarthy

He smiles like a Christian with four aces.

Bill Moyers

Depression is when you are out of work. A recession is when your neighbor is out of work. A recovery is when Jimmy Carter is out of work.

Ronald Reagan

Carter is the best president the Soviet Union ever had.

William Safire

Henry Clay *(1777–1852)*
He said, "I would rather be right than be president." This was the sourest grape since Aesop originated his fable.

Irving Stone

Grover Cleveland *(1837–1908)*
A man of force and stubbornness with no breadth of view, no training in our history and traditions, and essentially coarse fibered and self-sufficient.

Henry Cabot Lodge

Bill Clinton *(b 1946)*
Slick Willie.

Anonymous

The Prince of Sleaze.

Jerry Brown (1992)

I have never seen . . . so slippery, so disgusting a candidate.

> *Nat Hentoff,*
> *'The Village Voice' (1992)*

Calvin Coolidge   *(1872–1933)*
He is so silent that he is always worth listening to.

> *Anonymous*

Calvin Coolidge's perpetual expression was of smelling something burning on the stove.

> *Sherwin L. Cook*

The greatest man who ever came out of Plymouth Corner, Vermont.

> *Clarence Darrow*

On his death—How can they tell?

> *Dorothy Parker*

Calvin Coolidge didn't say much, and when he did he didn't say much.

> *Will Rogers*

Thomas E. Dewey   *(1902-71)*
He is the nastiest little man I've ever known. He struts
along sitting down.

Mrs. Clarence Dykstra
(1952)

On Dewey's announcing his presidential candi-
dacy—Dewey has thrown his diaper into the ring.

Harold L. Ickes

I know Governor Thomas E. Dewey, and Mr. Dewey is
a fine man. Yes, Dewey is a fine man. So is my Uncle
Morris. My Uncle Morris shouldn't be president; neither
should Dewey.

George Jessel

Everett Dirksen   *(1896-1969)*
The Wizard of Ooze.

John F. Kennedy

Stephen A. Douglas   *(1813-61)*
His argument is as thin as the homeopathic soup that
was made by boiling the shadow of a pigeon that had
been starved to death.

Abraham Lincoln

He appears to have been called "The Little Giant" more because he was little than because he was a giant.

Irving Stone,
'They Also Ran'

John Foster Dulles *(1888–1959)*

A diplomatic bird of prey smelling out from afar the corpses of dead bodies.

James Cameron (1967)

Foster Dulles is the only case I know of a bull who carries a china shop with him.

Sir Winston Churchill

Smooth is an inadequate word for Dulles. His prevarications are so highly polished as to be aesthetically pleasurable.

I. F. Stone (1953)

Dwight D. Eisenhower *(1890–1969)*

As an intellectual, he bestowed upon the games of golf and bridge all the enthusiasm and perseverance that he withheld from his books and ideas.

Emmet John Hughes

If I talk over people's heads, Ike must talk under their feet.

Adlai Stevenson

Geraldine Ferraro *(b 1935)*

I can't say it, but it rhymes with rich.

Barbara Bush (1984)

(There followed an apology from Mrs. Bush—claiming she had meant "witch.")

Gerald Ford *(b 1913)*

Gerald Ford was unknown throughout America. Now he's unknown throughout the world.

Anonymous

Nixon impeached himself. He gave us Ford as his revenge.

Bella Abzug

He looks like the guy in the science fiction movie who is first to see "the creature."

David Frye

In the Bob Hope Golf Classic, the participation of President Gerald Ford was more than enough to remind you that the nuclear button was at one stage at the disposal of a man who might have either pressed it by mistake or else pressed it deliberately in order to obtain room service.

Clive James (1980)

Gerry Ford is a nice guy, but he played too much football with his helmet off.

Lyndon B. Johnson

He looks and talks like he just fell off Edgar Bergen's lap.

David Steinberg (1975)

Benjamin Franklin   *(1706-90)*
A crafty and lecherous old hypocrite whose very statue seems to gloat on the wenches as they walk the States House yard.

William Cobbett

Ulysses S. Grant   *(1822-85)*
The people are tired of a man who has not an idea above a horse or a cigar.

Joseph Brown (1871)

Early in 1869 there was a cry for "no politicians," but the country did not mean "no brains."

William Claflin (1870)

He combined great gifts with a great mediocrity.

Woodrow Wilson

Warren G. Harding   *(1865-1923)*
Everybody's second choice.

Anonymous

Few deaths are unmingled tragedies. Harding's was not;
he died in time.

Samuel Hopkins Adams

Harding was not a bad man. He was just a slob.

Alice Roosevelt Longworth

Benjamin Harrison   *(1833-1901)*
He is a cold-blooded, narrow-minded, prejudiced, obstinate, timid, old psalm-singing Indianapolis politician.

Theodore Roosevelt

Gary Hart   *(b 1937)*
Hart is Kennedy typed on the eighth carbon.

Lance Morrow (1987)

Q: What do Gary Hart and the Boston Celtics have in
common?
A: If they had played at home, they would have won.

'Playboy' (1988)

Patrick Henry   *(1736–99)*
All tongue, without either head or heart.

Thomas Jefferson

Herbert Hoover   *(1874–1964)*
Hoover isn't a stuffed shirt. But at times he can give the most convincing impersonation of a stuffed shirt you ever saw.

Anonymous

If you put a rose in Hoover's hand it would melt.

Gutzon Borglum

A private meeting with Hoover is like sitting in a bath of ink.

Henry Stimson

Such a little man could not have made so big a depression.

Norman Thomas (1960)

Hubert H. Humphrey   *(1911–1978)*
He talks so fast that listening to him is like trying to read 'Playboy' magazine with your wife turning the pages.

Barry Goldwater

Vice President Humphrey has no function in any game his government plays except to lead the cheers.

Murray Kempton (1966)

Thomas Jefferson   *(1743–1826)*
Jeffersonian Democracy simply meant the possession of the federal government by the agrarian masses led by an aristocracy of slave-owning planters.

Charles A. Beard

A sterile worshipper of the people.

John B. McCaster

Andrew Johnson   *(1808–75)*
His mind had one compartment for right and one for wrong but no middle chamber where the two could commingle.

Howard K. Beale

An insolent drunken brute, in comparison with whom Caligula's horse was respectable.

'New York World' (1865)

Lyndon B. Johnson *(1908–73)*
He did not suffer from a poor education; he suffered from the belief that he had a poor education.

> *George Ball*

He is a man of his most recent word.

> *William F. Buckley, Jr.,*
> *'National Review' (1965)*

Hyperbole was to Lyndon Johnson what oxygen is to life.

> *Bill Moyers (1969)*

A damn independent boy; independent as a hog on ice.

> *Sam Rayburn*

Edward Kennedy *(b 1932)*
Every country should have at least one King Farouk.

> *Gore Vidal (1981)*

John F. Kennedy *(1917–63)*
Kennedy after all has lots of glamour—Gregory Peck with an atom bomb in his holster.

> *William F. Buckley, Jr.,*
> *'National Review' (1963)*

His speaking style is pseudo-Roman: "Ask not what your country can do for you . . . " Why not say, "Don't ask . . . "? "Ask not . . . " is the style of a man playing the role of being president, not of a man being president.

> *Herb Gold,*
> *'New York Post' (1962)*

The enviably attractive nephew who sings an Irish ballad for the company and then winsomely disappears before the table clearing and dishwashing begin.

> *Lyndon B. Johnson*

It is said the president is willing to laugh at himself. That is fine. But when is he going to extend that privilege to us?

> *Mort Sahl*

Robert Kennedy *(1925–68)*

Bobby Kennedy and Nelson Rockefeller are having a row, ostensibly over the plight of New York's mentally retarded, a loose definition of which would include everyone in New York who voted for Kennedy or Rockefeller.

> *William F. Buckley, Jr.,*
> *'National Review' (1966)*

Henry Kissinger   *(b 1923)*
An eel icier than ice.

Oriana Fallaci

When Kissinger can get the Nobel Peace Prize, what is there left for satire?

Tom Lehrer

Ed Koch   *(b 1924)*
I think he is an entertainer. I would prefer him to be a performer.

Carol Bellamy (1985)

'Mayor'—It's the greatest love story since 'Tristan and Isolde', and Ed Koch plays both parts.

Daniel Wolf,
'Daily Telegraph' (1984)

Fiorello La Guardia   *(1882-1947)*
If it's La Guardia or bust, I prefer bust.

Joseph M. Price

Abraham Lincoln   *(1804-65)*
His mind works in the right directions but seldom works clearly and cleanly. His bread is of unbolted flour, and much straw, too, mixes in the bran, and sometimes gravel stones.

Henry Ward Beecher

We did not conceive it possible that even Mr. Lincoln would produce a paper [The Gettysburg Address] so slipshod, so loose-jointed, so puerile, not alone in literary construction, but in its ideals, its sentiments, its grasp. He has outdone himself. Has literally come out of the little end of his own horn. By the side of it, mediocrity is superb.

'Chicago Times' (1863)

Henry Cabot Lodge   *(1902-85)*

He was as cool as an undertaker at a hanging.

H. L. Mencken (1920)

He considers himself so far superior to the ordinary run of people that the mere addition of another enemy to his long string means nothing to him one way or another.

*'Saturday Evening Post'
(1910)*

Huey Long   *(1893-1935)*

He was a liar, and he was nothing but a damn demagogue. It didn't surprise me when they shot him.

Harry S. Truman

Eugene McCarthy *(b 1916)*

He is meticulously liberal—never ever has he erred in the direction of common sense, when the alternative was to vote liberal.

William F. Buckley, Jr.,
'On the Right' (1967)

Joseph McCarthy *(1908–57)*

The only major politician in the country who can be labeled "liar" without fear of libel.

Joseph and Stewart Alsop
(1953)

He was nothing but a damn coward.

Harry S. Truman

William McKinley *(1843–1901)*

Why, if a man were to call my dog McKinley, and the brute failed to resent to the death the damning insult, I'd drown it.

William Cowper Brann

McKinley shows all the backbone of a chocolate eclair.

Theodore Roosevelt

Walter Mondale   *(b 1928)*
His [presidential] campaign kickoff was so dismal that it needed a plastic surgeon instead of a press agent to put a face on it.

Jane Mayer, 'Wall Street Journal' (1984)

Richard M. Nixon   *(b 1913)*
Dick is a four-letter word.

Democratic campaign slogan

Where is Lee Harvey Oswald now that his country needs him?

Graffiti

He told us he was going to take crime out of the streets. He did. He took it into the damn White House.

Ralph Abernathy

Nixon is a purposeless man, but I have great faith in his cowardice.

Jimmy Breslin

I wouldn't trust Nixon from here to that phone.

Barry Goldwater, 'Newsweek' (1986)

Avoid all needle drugs—the only dope worth shooting is Richard Nixon.

Abbie Hoffman (1971)

Sir Richard-the-Chicken-Hearted.

Hubert H. Humphrey

On a Nixon speech—I may not know much, but I know chicken shit from chicken salad.

Lyndon B. Johnson

Last Thursday Mr. Nixon dismissed me as "another Truman." I regard this as a compliment. I consider him another Dewey.

John F. Kennedy

Would you buy a second-hand car from this man?

Mort Sahl

He is the kind of politician who would cut down a redwood tree, then mount the stump for a conservation speech.

Adlai Stevenson

Franklin Pierce   *(1804–69)*
Many persons have difficulty remembering what President Franklin Pierce is best remembered for, and he is therefore probably best forgotten.

Richard Armour

James K. Polk   *(1795–1849)*
A victim of the use of water as a beverage.

Sam Houston

J. Danforth (Dan) Quayle   *(b 1947)*
An empty suit that goes to funerals and plays golf.

H. Ross Perot (1992)

Ronald Reagan   *(b 1911)*
Q: What ever happened to Rosemary's Baby?
A: He's in the White House.

Graffiti

Ronald Reagan couldn't be here tonight; he's posing for the cover of 'Guns and Ammo.'

Johnny Carson

You don't have to be smart to act—look at the outgoing President of the United States.

Cher, 'Playboy' (1988)

I'm glad that Reagan is president. Of course, I'm a professional comedian.

Will Durst

I listen to Reagan and I want to throw up.

Henry Fonda (1981)

That youthful sparkle in his eye is caused by his contact lenses, which he keeps highly polished.

Sheila Graham, 'The (London) Times' (1981)

I believe that Ronald Reagan can make this country what it once was—an Arctic region covered with ice.

Steve Martin

Q: What do you get if you cross James Dean with Ronald Reagan?
A: A rebel without a clue.

'Playboy' (1988)

Reagan is proof that there is life after death.

Mort Sahl

Washington could not tell a lie; Nixon could not tell the truth; Reagan cannot tell the difference.

Mort Sahl

A working man voting for Reagan is like a chicken voting for Colonel Sanders.

Paul Sarbanes

We've got the kind of president who thinks arms control means some kind of deodorant.

Patricia Schroeder

A triumph of the embalmer's art.

Gore Vidal

I think that Nancy does most of his talking; you'll notice that she never drinks water when Ronnie speaks.

Robin Williams (1982)

Franklin D. Roosevelt *(1882–1945)*
The best newspaperman who has ever been President
of the United States.

> *Heywood Broun*

I'd rather be right than be Roosevelt.

> *Heywood Broun*

He would rather follow public opinion than lead it.

> *Harry Hopkins*

The man who started more creations that were ever
begun since Genesis—and finished none.

> *Hugh Johnson (1937)*

Two-thirds mush and one-third Eleanor.

> *Alice Roosevelt Longworth*

If he became convinced tomorrow that coming out for
cannibalism would get him the votes he sorely needs,
he would begin fattening a missionary in the White
House backyard come Wednesday.

> *H. L. Mencken*

Theodore Roosevelt *(1859-1919)*
If there's one thing for which I admire you, it's your original discovery of the Ten Commandments.

Thomas B. Reed

My father always wanted to be the corpse at every funeral, the bride at every wedding, and the baby at every christening.

Alice Roosevelt Longworth

Adlai Stevenson *(1900-65)*
Unexceptional as a glass of decent Beaujolais.

'Newsweek' (1965)

Stevenson himself hasn't even backbone training, for he is a graduate of Dean Acheson's spineless school of diplomacy, which cost the free world six hundred million former allies in the past seven years of Trumanism.

Richard M. Nixon (1952)

The real trouble with Stevenson is that he's no better than a regular sissy.

Harry S. Truman

Adlai Stevenson was a man who could never make up his mind whether he had to go to the bathroom or not.

Harry S. Truman

Robert A. Taft   *(1889-1953)*
He has a positive genius for being wrong. He is an authentic living representative of the old Bourbons of whom it was said that they "learned nothing, forgot nothing."

Marvin Harrison,
'Robert A. Taft: Our
Illustrious Dunderhead'

The Dagwood Bumstead of American Politics.

'Time' (1940)

Zachary Taylor   *(1784-1850)*
Old Rough and Ready!

Nickname

Quite ignorant for his rank, and quite bigoted in his ignorance.

Winfield Scott, 'Memoirs'

Harry S. Truman   *(1884-1972)*
The two-bit president of a five-star general.

Anonymous

Among President Truman's many weaknesses was his utter inability to discriminate between history and histrionics.

Anonymous

To err is Truman.

Republican slogan

He is a man totally unfitted for the position. His principles are elastic, and he is careless with the truth. He has no special knowledge of any subject, and he is a malignant, scheming sort of an individual.

John L. Lewis (1948)

Harry Truman proves the old adage that any man can become President of the United States.

Norman Thomas

Gore Vidal   (b 1925)
Mr. Gore Vidal, the playwright and quipster who lost a Congressional race a few years ago but continues to seek out opportunities to advertise his ignorance of contemporary affairs.

William F. Buckley, Jr.,
'On the Right' (1964)

George Wallace   (b 1919)
I don't think you'll have to worry that this mental midget, this hillbilly Hitler from Alabama, is anywhere near becoming the nominee of the Democratic Party.

Julian Bond

George Washington   *(1732-99)*
That Washington was not a scholar is certain. That he is too illiterate, unlearned, unread for his station and reputation is equally beyond dispute.

John Adams (1782)

Woodrow Wilson   *(1856-1924)*
President Wilson indeed came to office with a noble message of hope, but unhappily in the sequel, hope proved to be his main equipment.

Lord Birkenhead

A sleepy man from a sleepy college [Princeton] in a sleepy little town.

Nicholas M. Butler

Mr. Wilson bores me with his Fourteen Points; why, God Almighty has only ten.

Georges Clemenceau

Mr. Wilson's mind, as has been the custom, will be closed all day Sunday.

George S. Kaufman

The air currents of the world never ventilated his mind.

Walter H. Page

12
THE MILITARY

GENERAL

It is the blood of the soldier that makes the general great.

Anonymous

A paratrooper is a man who descends from trees he did not climb.

Anonymous

Join the Army, see the world, meet interesting people—and kill them.

Pacifist reply to army recruitment poster

Make love, not war.

Pacifist slogan

Ban the bomb.

Pacifist slogan

Better Red than dead.

Pacifist slogan

Bombing can end the war: bomb the Pentagon now!

*Pacifist slogan during the
Vietnam War*

War is the science of destruction.

John Abbott

I have never understood this liking for war. It panders to instincts already catered for within the scope of any respectable domestic establishment.

*Alan Bennett,
'Forty Years On' (1968)*

I am convinced that the best service a retired general can perform is to turn in his tongue along with his suit and to mothball his opinions.

Gen. Omar Bradley (1959)

There are no warlike peoples—just warlike leaders.

Ralph Bunche

There is nothing that war has ever achieved that we could not have better achieved without it.

Havelock Ellis

It takes fifteen thousand casualties to train a major-general.

Ferdinand Foch

There never was a good war or a bad peace.

Benjamin Franklin

The draft is white people sending black people to fight yellow people to protect the country they stole from red people.

*Gerome Gragni and
James Rado (1967)*

War is death's feast.

George Herbert

Older men declare war. But it is the youth that must fight and die.

Herbert Hoover (1944)

What is absurd and monstrous about war is that men who have no personal quarrel should be trained to murder one another in cold blood.

Aldous Huxley

Better to live in peace than to begin war and lie dead.

Chief Joseph

The first advice I am going to give my successor is to watch the generals and to avoid feeling that just because they were military men their opinions on military matters were worth a damn.

John F. Kennedy

Military intelligence is a contradiction in terms.

Groucho Marx

Military justice is to justice what military music is to music.

Groucho Marx

War will never cease until babies begin to come into the world with larger cerebrums and smaller adrenals.

H. L. Mencken

No one hates war more than he who has seen a lot of it.

Richard Nixon (1959)

You can't say civilization don't advance—for every war they kill you a new way.   *Will Rogers*

Sometime they'll give a war and nobody will come.

Carl Sandburg,
'The People, Yes' (1936)

War is much too serious to be left to military men.

Charles M. Talleyrand

The Pentagon—A place where costs are always rounded to the nearest tenth of a billion dollars.

C. Merton Tyrrell (1970)

MILITARY LEADERS

General George Custer   *(1836-76)*
He has gone down in history as the man who blew the Little Big Horn.
Anonymous

Alexander Haig   *(b 1924)*
One thing I don't want around me is an intellectual military. I don't have to worry about you on that score.

Henry Kissinger

Captain Barney Kelly
After he allowed the USS Enterprise to run aground in San Francisco Bay—He grounds the warship he walks on.

John Bracken (1983)

General Douglas MacArthur   *(1880–1964)*
I studied dramatics under him for twelve years.

Dwight D. Eisenhower

MacArthur is the type of man who thinks that when he gets to heaven, God will step down from the great white throne and bow him into His vacated seat.

Harold Ickes,
'Diary' (1933)

I fired him because he wouldn't respect the authority of the president. I didn't fire him because he was a dumb son-of-a-bitch, although he was, but that's not against the law for generals. If it was, half to three-quarters of them would be in jail.

Harry S. Truman

General George B. McClellan *(1826–85)*
My dear McClellan,

If you don't want to use the army, I should like to borrow it for a while.

Yours respectfully,
Abraham Lincoln

Field-Marshal B. L. Montgomery *(1887–1976)*
In defeat he was unbeatable; in victory, unbearable.

Edward Marsh

General George S. Patton, Jr. *(1885–1945)*
Patton was an acolyte to Mars.

Col. F. Farley (1964)

Saddam Hussein *(b 1937)*
Saddam Insane is the SCUD of the Earth!

Colin M. Jarman (1991)

As far as Saddam Hussein being a great military strategist, he is neither a strategist nor is he schooled in operational arts. He's not a tactician. He's not a general. He's not a soldier. Other than that, he's a great military man.
Gen. H. Norman
Schwarzkopf (1991)

13
FOOD AND DRINK

Appetizers are those little bits you eat until you lose
your appetite.

Anonymous

If the soup had been as hot as the claret, if the claret
had been as old as the bird, and if the bird's breasts had
been as full as the waitress's, it would have been a very
good dinner.

Anonymous

Eating food with a knife and fork is like making love
through an interpreter.

Anonymous

A prune is a plum that has seen better days.

Anonymous

A raisin is a worried-looking grape.

Anonymous

Bagels are made with love and a little cement.

Anonymous

Vegetables are substances used by children to balance their plate while carrying it to and from the dining table.

Anonymous

You are what you eat.

Anonymous

Alcohol is a liquid that can put the wreck into recreation.

Anonymous

English cooking—You just put things in hot water and take them out again after a while.

Anonymous French chef

Never eat in a place called "Mom's."

Nelson Algren

Three million frogs' legs are served in Paris—daily. Nobody knows what became of the rest of the frogs.

Fred Allen

I will not eat oysters. I want my food dead—not sick, not wounded—dead.

Woody Allen

Murder is commoner among cooks than among members of any other profession.

W. H. Auden (1973)

Chinese food—You do not sew with a fork and I see no reason why you should eat with knitting needles.

Henry Beard (1981)

Clams—I simply cannot imagine why anyone would eat something slimy served in an ashtray.

Henry Beard (1981)

Be content to remember that those who can make omelettes properly can do nothing else.

Hilaire Belloc

Drinking makes such fools of people, and people are such fools to begin with that it's compounding a felony.

Robert Benchley

A cabbage is a familiar kitchen-garden vegetable about as large and wise as a man's head.

Ambrose Bierce

A chop is a piece of leather skillfully attached to a bone and administered to the patients at restaurants.

Ambrose Bierce

The local groceries are all out of broccoli,
                    Loccoli.

Ray Blount, Jr.,
'Atlantic Monthly'

Those magazine dieting stories always have the testimonial of a woman who wore a dress that could slip-cover New Jersey in one photo and thirty days later looked like a well-dressed thermometer.

Erma Bombeck

I've been on a constant diet for the last two decades. I've lost a total of 789 pounds. By all accounts, I should be hanging from a charm bracelet.

Erma Bombeck

Desserts remain for a moment or two in your mouth
and for the rest of your life on your hips.

> *Peg Bracken,*
> *'The I Hate to Cook Book'*

*(More popularly: A moment on your lips, a lifetime on your
hips.)*

Vegetarianism—You are what you eat, and who wants
to be a lettuce?

> *Peter Burns (1984)*

Beer is not a good cocktail party drink, especially in a
home where you don't know where the bathroom is.

> *Billy Carter (1977)*

Cold duck—A carbonated wine foisted upon Americans (who else would drink it?) by winery ad agencies
as a way of getting rid of inferior champagne by mixing
it with inferior burgundy.

> *John Ciardi (1983)*

Pâté—Nothing more than a French meat loaf that's had
a couple of cocktails.

> *Carol Cutler*

Most vigitaryans I iver see looked enough like their
food to be classed as cannybals.

> *Finley Peter Dunne (1900)*

My illness is due to my doctor's insistence that I drink milk, a whitish fluid they force down helpless babies.

W. C. Fields

I did not say that this meat was tough. I just said I didn't see the horse that usually stands outside.

W. C. Fields (1941)

Alcohol may pick you up a little bit, but it sure lets you down in a hurry.

Betty Ford (1979)

The food here is so tasteless you could eat a meal of it and belch and it wouldn't remind you of anything.

Redd Foxx

A gourmet is just a glutton with brains.

Philip W. Gaberman, Jr., 'Vogue' (1961)

I have known many meat eaters to be far more nonviolent than vegetarians.

Mohandas Gandhi (1948)

Airline Meals

Anything that's white is sweet.
Anything that's brown is meat.
Anything that's gray don't eat.

Hermione Gingold

As for butter versus margarine, I trust cows more than chemists.

Joan Gussow (1986)

The worst drug of today is not smack or pot—it's refined sugar.

George Hamilton (1980)

Show me a nation whose national beverage is beer, and I'll show you an advanced toilet technology.

Paul Hawkins (1977)

I'm frightened of eggs, worse than frightened, they revolt me. That white round thing without any holes. Have you ever seen anything more revolting than an egg yolk breaking and spilling its yellow liquid? Blood is jolly, red. But egg yolk is yellow, revolting. I've never tasted it.

Alfred Hitchcock (1963)

I like liquor—its taste and effects—and that is just the reason why I never drink it.

Thomas "Stonewall"
Jackson

One of the disadvantages of wine is that it makes a man mistake words for thoughts.

Samuel Johnson

If you have formed the habit of checking on every new diet that comes along, you will find that, mercifully, they all blur together, leaving you with only one definite piece of information—french fried potatoes are out.

Jean Kerr, 'Please Don't
Eat the Daisies' (1957)

She ate so many clams that her stomach rose and fell with the tide.

Louis Kronenberger,
'The Cutting Edge'

Brandy and water spoils two good things.

Charles Lamb

Large, naked, raw carrots are acceptable as food only to those who live in hutches eagerly awaiting Easter.

Fran Lebowitz

Only Irish coffee provides in a single glass all four essential food groups—alcohol, caffeine, sugar, and fat.

Alex Levine

A man takes a drink, the drink takes another, and the drink takes the man.

Sinclair Lewis

Never eat Chinese food in Oklahoma.

Bryan Miller

The trouble with eating Italian food is that five or six days later you're hungry again.

George Miller

Americans can eat garbage, provided you sprinkle it liberally with ketchup, mustard, chili sauce, Tabasco sauce, cayenne pepper, or any other condiment which destroys the original flavor of the dish.

Henry Miller, 'Remember to Remember' (1947)

After being served matzo ball soup three days in a row—Isn't there any other part of the matzo you can eat?

Marilyn Monroe

Vegetarians have wicked, shifty eyes and laugh in a cold, calculating manner. They pinch little children, steal stamps, drink water, favor beards.

J. B. Morton,
'Daily Express'

I understand the big food companies are developing a tearless onion. I think they can do it—after all, they've already given us tasteless bread.

Robert Orben

Remember the days when you let your child have some chocolate if he finished his cereal? Now, chocolate is one of the cereals.

Robert Orben

Nutrition makes me puke.

Jimmy Piersall

Health food may be good for the conscience but Oreos taste a hell of a lot better.

Robert Redford

You can't barbecue in New York; you'd have to keep vacuuming the meat.

"Rhoda," CBS-TV

Refusing an invitation to a vegetarian dinner—The thought of two thousand people crunching celery at the same time horrified me.

George Bernard Shaw

If the English can survive their food, they can survive anything.

George Bernard Shaw

In Mexico we have a word for sushi—bait.

José Simon

Remember the good old days when a liquid-protein diet was chicken soup?

Gil Stern

It's a naive domestic Burgundy without any breeding, but I think you'll be amused by its presumption.

James Thurber (1943)

I never eat in a restaurant that's over a hundred feet off the ground and won't stand still.

Calvin Trillin (1979)

They served haggis at the last dinner I attended. I didn't know whether to kick it or eat it. Having eaten it, I wished I'd have kicked it.

Stuart Turner

The Germans are exceedingly fond of Rhine wines. One tells them from the vinegar by the label.

Mark Twain (1880)

A few years ago it was considered chic to serve Beef Wellington; fortunately, like Napoleon, it met its Waterloo.

Rene Veaux

There must be some good in the cocktail party to account for its immense vogue among otherwise sane people.

Evelyn Waugh

Gluttony is not a secret vice.

Orson Welles

My wife is on a diet. Coconuts and bananas. She hasn't lost any weight, but she can sure climb a tree.

Henny Youngman

14
THE WORLD

AUSTRALIA

Australia is a big blank map, and the whole people is constantly sitting over it like a committee, trying to work out the best way to fill it in.

Charles E. W. Bean

You don't say "Cheers" when you drink a cup of tea in the bush; you say, "Christ, the flies!"

Prince Charles

To live in Australia permanently is rather like going to a party and dancing all night with one's mother.

Barry Humphries (1976)

AUSTRIA

Austria is Switzerland speaking pure German and with history added.

J. E. Morpugo,
'The Road to Athens'

CANADA

If the mental illness of the United States is megalomania, that of Canada is paranoid schizophrenia.

Margaret Atwood

A Canadian is a person who knows how to make love in a canoe.

Pierre Berton

Perhaps the most striking thing about Canada is that it is not part of the United States.

J. Bartlet Brebner

A country so square that even the female impersonators are women.

Richard Brenner

You have to know a man awfully well in Canada to know his surname.

John Buchan

The beaver is a good national symbol for Canada. He's so busy chewing he can't see what's going on.

Howard Cable

I don't even know what street Canada is on.

Al Capone

Canada could have enjoyed: English government, French culture, and American know-how. Instead it ended up with: English know-how, French government, and American culture.

John R. Colombo,
'Oh Canada' (1965)

Canada is the boring second fiddle in the American symphony.

Andrey Gromyko (1955)

Canada's national bird is the grouse.

Stuart Keate

Very little is known of the Canadian country since it's rarely visited by anyone but the Queen and illiterate sports fishermen.

P. J. O'Rourke, 'National Lampoon' (1976)

Canadians are generally indistinguishable from Americans, and the surest way of telling the two apart is to make the observation to a Canadian.

Richard Staines

CHINA

Chinese is a language of fifteen thousand words and none of them in English.

Anonymous

DENMARK

Beer is the Danish national drink, and the Danish national weakness is another beer.

Clementine Paddleford (1964)

ENGLAND

An Englishman will burn his bed to catch a flea.

Turkish proverb

The English have no exalted sentiments. They can all be bought.

Napoleon Bonaparte

The most dangerous thing in the world is to make a friend of an Englishman, because he'll come sleep in your closet rather than spend ten shillings on a hotel.

Truman Capote

The English never draw a line without blurring it.

Sir Winston Churchill

The English think incompetence is the same thing as sincerity.

Quentin Crisp

An Englishman is a man who lives on an island in the North Sea governed by Scotsmen.

Philip Guedella,
'Supers and Superman'

Silence can be defined as conversation with an Englishman.

Heinrich Heine

I am firmly convinced that a blaspheming Frenchman is a spectacle more pleasing to the Lord than a praying Englishman.

Heinrich Heine

In dealing with Englishmen you can be sure of one thing only, that the logical solution will not be adopted.

William Inge

The English are so bloody nosy.

Elton John

In order to appreciate England one has to have a certain contempt for logic.

Lin Yutang

Three things to beware of—The hoof of a horse, the horn of a bull, and the smile of an Englishman.

Seamus MacManus

When it's three o'clock in New York, it's still 1938 in London.

Bette Midler (1978)

The English are always ready to admire anything so long as they can queue up.

> George Mikes,
> 'How to Be an Alien'

What distinguishes Cambridge from Oxford, broadly speaking, is that nobody who has been to Cambridge feels impelled to write about it.

> A. A. Milne

An Englishman is a creature who thinks he is being virtuous when he is only being uncomfortable.

> George Bernard Shaw

The English are a nation of shopkeepers.

> Adam Smith,
> 'The Wealth of Nations'

I did a picture in England one winter and it was so cold I almost got married.

> Shelley Winters

The English have an extraordinary ability for flying into a great calm.

> Alexander Woollcott

FRANCE

Paris is a disease; sometimes it is several diseases.

Honoré de Balzac

The French complain about everything and always.

*Napoleon Bonaparte
(1804)*

The simple thing is to consider the French as an erratic and brilliant people, who have all the gifts except that of running their country.

*James Cameron, 'News
Chronicle' (1954)*

Paris is a great city of gaieties and pleasures, where four-fifths of the inhabitants die of grief.

Nicholas de Chamfort

The largest country in Europe, a great boon for drunks who need room to fall.

*Alan Coren, 'The Sanity
Inspector' (1974)*

There has always been something fishy about the French.

Noël Coward,
'Conversation Piece'

To err is human, to loaf Parisian.

Victor Hugo,
'Les Misérables' (1862)

If you're going to Paris you would do well to remember this: no matter how politely or distinctly you ask a Parisian a question he will persist in answering you in French.

Fran Lebowitz

The French are sawed-off sissies who eat snails and slugs and cheese that smells like people's feet. Utter cowards who force their own children to drink wine, they gibber like baboons even when you try to speak to them in their own wimpy language.

P. J. O'Rourke, 'National Lampoon' (1976)

The only country where the money falls apart and you can't tear the toilet paper.

Billy Wilder

GERMANY

The German mind has a talent for making no mistakes
but the very greatest.

Clifton Fadiman

Germans abroad are no better than exported beer.

Heinrich Heine

One German makes a philosopher, two a public meeting, three a war.

Robert MacDonald,
'Summit Conference'
(1982)

Everything ponderous, viscous, and solemnly clumsy,
all long-winded and boring types of style are developed
in profuse variety among Germans.

Friedrich Nietzsche (1886)

German is the most extravagantly ugly language—it
sounds like someone using a sick bag on a 747.

Willy Rushton (1984)

Whenever the literary German dives into a sentence, that is the last you are going to see of him till he emerges on the other side of the Atlantic with his verb in his mouth.

*Mark Twain, 'A
Connecticut Yankee in King
Arthur's Court' (1889)*

The great virtues of the German people have created more evils than idleness ever did vices.

Paul Valéry (1924)

GREECE

After shaking hands with a Greek, count your fingers.

Albanian proverb

The Greeks—dirty and impoverished descendants of a bunch of la-de-da fruit salads who invented democracy and then forgot how to use it while walking around dressed up like girls.

*P. J. O'Rourke, 'National
Lampoon' (1976)*

HUNGARY

If you have a Hungarian for a friend you don't need any enemies.

Hungarian proverb

INDIA

India is a geographical term. It is no more a united nation than the equator.

Sir Winston Churchill

IRELAND

What's Dublin? Can you play it?

Louis Armstrong

The Irish are a very popular race—with themselves.

Brendan Behan

An Anglo-Irishman is a Protestant with a horse.

Brendan Behan,
'The Hostage'

The quiet Irishman is about as harmless as a powder magazine built over a match factory.

James Dunne

The Irish people do not gladly suffer common sense.

Oliver St. John Gogarty
(1935)

The Irish are a fair people: they never speak well of one another.

Samuel Johnson

The old sow that eats her farrow.

James Joyce

Italy, at least, has two things to balance its miserable poverty and mismanagement: a lively intellectual movement and a good climate. Ireland is Italy without these two.

James Joyce (1906)

The trouble with Ireland is that it's a country full of genius, but with absolutely no talent.

Hugh Leonard

ITALY

Venice—The only place where you can get seasick by crossing the street.

Anonymous

Telegram from Venice to his editor—Streets flooded. Please advise.

Robert Benchley

Except for white truffles, pasta, and opera, the Italians cannot be credited with anything.

Pierre Berge

Italy is a paradise for horses, a hell for women.

Robert Burton (1621)

Venice—A city for beavers.

Ralph Waldo Emerson, 'Journal' (1833)

A poor country full of rich people.

Richard Gardner

Venice would be a fine city if it were only drained.

Ulysses S. Grant (1879)

JAPAN

The Japanese are a people with a genius for doing anything they set out to do as a matter of national decision.

George Ball,
'Newsweek' (1975)

Are extremely good imitators—and so polite they even copy the mistakes.

Earl Scruggs (1968)

The Japanese have perfected good manners and made them indistinguishable from rudeness.

Paul Theroux

LUXEMBOURG

On a clear day you can't see Luxembourg at all. This is because a tree is in the way.

Alan Coren, 'The Sanity
Inspector' (1974)

MEXICO

Mexico should adopt the cactus as its national flower.

'Grand Rapids Herald'

A country where men despise sex, and live for it.

D. H. Lawrence

THE MIDDLE EAST

The Middle East is where oil is thicker than water.

James Holland

RUSSIA

Russia scares me—the people on the buses are so serious they look like they're going to the electric chair.

Muhammad Ali (1978)

A riddle wrapped in a mystery inside an enigma.

Sir Winston Churchill

Probably the most boring country in the history of nations.

Norman Mailer (1968)

Russia is a country that buries its troubles. Your criticism is your epitaph. You simply say your say, and then you're through.

Will Rogers

SCOTLAND

There are few more impressive sights in the world than a Scotsman on the make.

J. M. Barrie

I have been trying all my life to like Scotchmen and am obliged to desist from the experiment in despair.

Charles Lamb

Their fumbled attempt at speaking the English language has been a source of amusement for five centuries, and their idiot music has been dreaded by those not blessed with deafness for at least as long.

P. J. O'Rourke, 'National Lampoon' (1976)

It requires a surgical operation to get a joke well into Scotch understanding.

Sydney Smith

That garret of the earth—that knuckle-end of England—that land of Calvin, oatcakes, and sulphur.

Sydney Smith

Had Cain been a Scot, God would have changed his
    doom;
Not forced him to wander, but confined him home.

Sydney Smith

SPAIN

Three Spaniards, four opinions.

Spanish proverb

A country that has sold its soul for cement and petrol and can only be saved by a series of earthquakes.

Cyril Connolly

Spain imports tourists and exports chambermaids.

Carlos Fuentes

SWEDEN

The Swedes have their medical expenses taken care of, all of their welfare costs paid for, their rent subsidized, and so much done for them, that if they lose their car keys they promptly commit suicide.

Godfrey Cambridge

SWITZERLAND

It is a curst, selfish, swinish country of brutes placed in the most romantic region of the world.

Lord Byron

The Swiss are not a people so much as a neat, clean, quiet, solvent business.

William Faulkner

A country where very few things begin, but many things end.

F. Scott Fitzgerald

A nation of money-grabbing clockmakers.

Nick Lowe (1978)

The Swiss are a neat and industrious people, none of whom is under seventy-five years of age. They make cheeses, milk chocolate, and watches, all of which, when you come right down to it, are fairly unnecessary.

> *Dorothy Parker,*
> *'The New Yorker' (1931)*

In Italy for thirty years under the Borgias, they had warfare, terror, murder, bloodshed. They produced Michelangelo, Leonardo da Vinci, and the Renaissance. In Switzerland, they had brotherly love, five hundred years of democracy and peace, and what did they produce? The cuckoo clock.

> *Orson Welles,*
> *'The Third Man' (1949)*

THE UNITED STATES

If you can speak three languages—you're trilingual. If you can speak two languages—you're bilingual. If you can only speak one language—you're an American.

> *Anonymous*

If God had meant for Texans to ski, he would have
made bullshit white.

Anonymous

His great aim was to escape from civilization, and, as
soon as he had money, he went to southern California.

Anonymous

California is so wonderful—on a clear day when the fog
lifts, you can see the smog.

Anonymous

California is the only place where you can have all four
seasons in one day.

Anonymous

The first thing that strikes a stranger in the Big Apple is
a taxicab.

Anonymous

I have just returned from Boston. It is the only thing to
do if you find yourself up there.

Fred Allen

New York has absolutely everything except a past.

Louis Auchinloss

The more I observed Washington, the more frequently I visited it, and the more people I interviewed there, the more I understood how prophetic L'Enfant was when he laid it out as a city that goes around in circles.

John Mason Brown

America is the best half-educated country in the world.

Nicholas M. Butler

The Americans are a funny lot; they drink whisky to keep them warm; then they put ice in it to make it cool; they put some sugar in it to make it sweet, and then they put a slice of lemon in it to make it sour. Then they say "Here's to you" and drink it themselves.

B. N. Chakravarty (1966)

Americans think of themselves as a huge rescue squad on twenty-four-hour call to any spot on the globe where dispute and conflict may erupt.

Eldridge Cleaver

America is where you can become a blueblood simply by having more greenbacks.

Bill Copeland

Philadelphia is not a town; it's a jungle. They don't have gyms there; they have zoos. They don't have sparring sessions; they have wars.

Angelo Dundee

Everything in L.A. is too large, too loud, and usually banal in concept. The plastic asshole of the world.

William Faulkner

Americans are like a rich father who wishes he knew how to give his sons the hardships that made him rich.

Robert Frost

This is the only country in the world where businessmen get together over twenty-dollar steaks to discuss hard times.

Honey Greer

This will never be a civilized country until we spend more money for books than we do on chewing gum.

Elbert Hubbard

The American has no language. He has dialect, slang, provincialism, accent, and so forth.

Rudyard Kipling

Thanks to the interstate highway system, it is now possible to travel from coast to coast without seeing anything.

Charles Kuralt

Americans are people who laugh at African witch doctors and spend 100 million dollars on fake reducing systems.

L. L. Levinson

There's nothing wrong with southern California that a rise in the ocean level wouldn't cure.

Ross MacDonald

A car is useless in New York, essential everywhere else. The same with good manners.

Mignon McLaughlin (1966)

Nobody ever went broke underestimating the taste of the American public.

H. L. Mencken

America's dissidents are not committed to mental hospitals and sent into exile; they thrive and prosper and buy a house in Nantucket and take flyers in the commodities market.

Ted Morgan, 'On Becoming an American' (1978)

The Bronx?
No, thonx!

Ogden Nash,
'The New Yorker' (1931)

Nothing important has ever come out of San Francisco,
Rice-A-Roni aside.

Michael O'Donoghue

A country that has leapt from barbarism to decadence
without touching civilization.

John O'Hara

America is a country that doesn't know where it is
going but is determined to set a speed record getting
there.

Laurence J. Peter

Here is the difference between Dante, Milton, and me.
They wrote about hell and never saw the place. I wrote
about Chicago after looking the town over for years
and years.

Carl Sandburg

If I owned Texas and Hell, I would rent out Texas and
live in Hell.

Gen. Philip H. Sheridan
(1855)

When it's 5 below in New York, it's 78 in Los Angeles, and when it's 110 in New York, it's 78 in Los Angeles. There are two million interesting people in New York, and only seventy-eight in Los Angeles.

Neil Simon (1979)

Of course America had often been discovered before Columbus, but it had always been hushed up.

Oscar Wilde

The thing that impresses me most about America is the way parents obey their children.

The Duke of Windsor

WALES

The Welsh are the only nation in the world that has produced no graphic or plastic art, no architecture, no drama. They just sing. Sing and blow down wind instruments of plated silver.

Evelyn Waugh,
'Decline and Fall' (1928)

15
THE SEXES

MEN

Women have their faults. Men have only two:
Everything they say. Everything they do.

Anonymous

If they can put one man on the moon, why can't they
put them all there?

Anonymous

Man is the missing link between the ape and the human being.

Anonymous

Adam came first, but men always do.

Anonymous

A gentleman is any man who wouldn't hit a woman with his hat on.

Fred Allen

The fastest way to a man's heart is through his chest.

Roseanne Arnold

I married beneath me. All women do.

Nancy Astor

Behind almost every woman you ever heard stands a man who let her down.

Naomi Bliven

God Created Adam—Then Corrected HER Mistake.

Brooklyn Women's
Bar Association

I refuse to consign the whole male sex to the nursery. I insist on believing that some men are my equals.

Brigid Brophy

The man is a domestic animal which, if treated with firmness and kindness, can be trained to do most things.

Jilly Cooper
'Cosmopolitan' (1972)

A man in love is incomplete until he has married. Then he's finished.

Zsa Zsa Gabor

A man is a creature with two legs and eight arms.

Jayne Mansfield

I require three things of a man. He must be handsome, ruthless, and stupid.

Dorothy Parker

A woman needs a man like a fish needs a bicycle.

Gloria Steinem

Why was man created on the last day? So that he can be told, when pride possesses him: God created the gnat before thee.

The Talmud

Man—a creature made at the end of the week's work when God was tired.

Mark Twain

Whatever women do they must do twice as well as men to be thought half as good. Luckily, this is not diffcult.

Charlotte Whitton

WOMEN

A man without a woman is like a neck without a pain.

Anonymous

Women have a passion for mathematics. They divide their age in half, double the price of their clothes, and always add at least five years to the age of their best friend.

Marcel Achard

A woman never sees what we do for her; she only sees what we don't do.

Georges Courteline

What men desire is a virgin who is a whore.

Edward Dahlberg,
'Reasons of the Heart'
(1965)

Women are like elephants to me; they're nice to look at but I wouldn't want to own one.

W. C. Fields

You don't know a woman until you've met her in court.

Norman Mailer

On one issue at least, men and women agree—they both distrust women.

H. L. Mencken

Men have more problems than women. In the first place, they have to put up with women.

Françoise Sagan

A woman reading 'Playboy' feels a little like a Jew reading a Nazi manual.

Gloria Steinem

Woman is generally so bad that the difference between a good and a bad woman scarcely exists.

Leo Tolstoy

God created man, and finding him not sufficiently alone, gave him a companion to make him feel his solitude more.

Paul Valéry,
'Tel Quel' (1943)

Women are made to be loved, not understood.

Oscar Wilde

SEX

The conventional position makes me claustrophobic. And the others either give me a stiff neck or lockjaw.

Tallulah Bankhead

I could be content that we might procreate like trees, without conjunction, or that there were any way to perpetuate the world without this trivial and vulgar way of coition: it is the foolishest act a wise man commits in all his life.

Thomas Browne (1642)

Sexual intercourse is a grossly overrated pastime; the positon is undignified, the pleasure momentary, and the consequences utterly damnable.

Lord Chesterfield

I think it's disgusting. Sex has always been with us, but never so flamboyantly as it is today. I was known as the "kissless star." My leading men used to say, "What's the matter with me—do I have bad breath?" I said, "No, but I'm against kissing on the screen." In a way, a kiss is a promise, and I didn't want to create the wrong impression.

Mary Pickford

16
INSULTS,
RETORTS, AND
SELF-CRITICISM

TARGET UNKNOWN

There are only two things I dislike about her—her face.

Anonymous

What he lacks in intelligence, he more than makes up for in stupidity.

Anonymous

His origins are so low, you'd have to limbo under his family tree.

Anonymous

The last time I saw him he was walking down Lovers' Lane holding his own hand.

Fred Allen

She's got such a narrow mind, when she walks fast her earrings bang together!

John Cantu

He has all the virtues I dislike and none of the vices I admire.

Winston Churchill

He left his body to science—and science is contesting the will.

David Frost

He must have had a magnificent build before his stomach went in for a career of its own.

Margaret Halsey

She felt in italics and thought in capitals.

Henry James

Her only flair is in her nostrils.

Pauline Kael

He is as good as his word—and his word is no good.

Seamus MacManus

I know she's outspoken, but by whom?

Dorothy Parker

The trouble with her is that she lacks the power of conversation but not the power of speech.

George Bernard Shaw

I don't like her. But don't misunderstand me: my dislike is purely platonic.

Sir Herbert Beerbohm Tree

His mother should have thrown him away and kept the stork.

Mae West

RETORTS

Anonymous actress: I enjoyed your book [*Past Imperfect*]. Who wrote it for you?
Ilka Chase: Darling, I'm so glad you liked it. Who read it to you?

Anonymous woman: There are two things I don't like about you, Mr. Churchill—your politics and your mustache.

Winston Churchill: My dear madam, pray do not disturb yourself. You are not likely to come into contact with either.

Anonymous woman: I've made a bet with a friend that I can get you to say at least three words this evening. What do you say to that?

Calvin Coolidge: You lose!

Anonymous singer: You know, my dear, I insured my voice for fifty thousand dollars.

Miriam Hopkins: That's wonderful. And what did you do with the money?

Anonymous writer: Last week you rejected my story. I know that you did not read it for, as a test, I pasted together pages fifteen, sixteen, and seventeen, and the manuscript came back with the pages still pasted. You are a fraud and you turn down stories without even reading them.

George Horace Latimer: Madam, at breakfast when I open an egg, I don't have to eat the whole egg to discover it is bad.

Lady Astor: Winston, if I were married to you, I'd put poison in your coffee.
Sir Winston Churchill: Nancy, if you were my wife, I'd drink it.

Tallulah Bankhead: How lucky you are to be married to Alfred Lunt, darling! His directing, his acting, his theater sense. Where would you be without him?
Lynne Fontaine: Probably playing your roles.

Winston Churchill: I venture to say that my Right Honorable friend, so redolent of other knowledge, knows nothing of farming. I'll even make a bet that she doesn't know how many toes a pig has!
Lady Astor: Oh, yes I do! Take off your little shoesies and have a look!

Henry Clay: I would rather be right than be president.
Congressman Reed: He doesn't have to worry. He'll never be either.

Isadora Duncan: Imagine a child with my body and your brain.
George Bernard Shaw: Yes, but suppose it had my body and your brain!

George Gershwin: If you had it all over again, would you fall in love with yourself again?
Oscar Levant: Play us a medley of your hit!

Ruth Gordon (*explaining her latest role*): There's no scenery at all. In the first scene, I'm on the left side of the stage and the audience has to imagine I'm eating dinner in a restaurant. Then in scene two, I run over to the right side of the stage, and the audience imagines I'm in the drawing room.

George S. Kaufman: And the second night, you have to imagine there's an audience out front.

Sir Edwin Landseer: How is it you never finish your work? I never understand artists who leave their paintings unfinished.

James McNeill Whistler: And I can never understand why you ever begin yours.

Clare Booth Luce (*on coming to a door*): Age before beauty.

Dorothy Parker (*sweeping through first*): Pearls before swine.

Lewis Morris (*on being overlooked for the poet laureateship*): It is a conspiracy of silence against me—a conspiracy of silence. What should I do?

Oscar Wilde: Join it!

Lord Sandwich: Really, Mr. Wilkes, I don't know whether you'll die on the gallows or of the pox.

John Wilkes: That depends, my Lord, on whether I embrace your principles or your mistress.

Oscar Wilde: Do you mind if I smoke?
Sarah Bernhardt: I don't care if you burn.

SELF-CRITICISM

Franklin P. Adams *(1881-1960)*
I am easily influenced. Compared with me a weather vane is Gibraltar.

Tallulah Bankhead *(1903-68)*
I'm as pure as the driven slush.

They used to photograph Shirley Temple through gauze. They should photograph me through linoleum.

Rona Barrett *(b 1936)*
I'm really a pussycat—with an iron tail.

Marlon Brando *(b 1924)*
I have eyes like those of a dead pig.

Agatha Christie *(1890-1976)*
A sausage machine, a perfect sausage.

George M. Cohan   *(1878-1942)*
I can write better plays than any living dancer and dance better than any living playwright.

Cyril Connolly   *(1903-74)*
I have always disliked myself at any given moment; the total of such moments is my life.

Calvin Coolidge   *(1873-1933)*
I think the American people want a solemn ass for president. And I think I'll go along with them.

Princess Diana   *(b 1961)*
I'm as thick as a plank.

Phyllis Diller   *(b 1917)*
If my jeans could talk they'd plead for mercy.

It's a good thing beauty is only skin deep, or I'd be rotten to the core.

Ernest Hemingway   *(1898-1961)*
As a war correspondent—I'm Ernie Hemorrhoid, the poor man's Pyle.

Charles Laughton   *(1899-1962)*
I have a face like the behind of an elephant.

Oscar Levant   *(1906–72)*
Under this flabby exterior is an enormous lack of character.

Groucho Marx   *(1898–1977)*
I don't wish to belong to any club that would want me as a member.

Golda Meir   *(1898–1978)*
I may not have been a great prime minister, but I would have been a great farmer.

David Niven   *(1910–83)*
I have a face that is a cross between two pounds of halibut and an explosion in an old clothes cupboard.

Joan Rivers   *(b 1937)*
I was so flat, I used to put X's on my chest and write, "You are here."

Kiri Te Kanawa   *(b 1944)*
I'm anorexic for an opera singer—but I'm a fat anorexic.

Mae West   *(1892–1980)*
I used to be Snow White, but I drifted.

INDEX